QUINSIGAMOND TALES, ETCETERA

A Memoir

by

IDAMAY MICHAUD ARSENAULT

GOOD NATURE PRESS

For further information, contact the author at:
Good Nature Press
9 Farmington Street
Worcester, MA 01603
IriteIclik@aol.com

Book design by:
The Floating Gallery
244 Madison Avenue, #254
New York, NY 10016-2819
(1-877) 822-2500

Quinsigamond Tales, Etcetera
by Idamay Michaud Arsenault
1. Author 2. Title 3. Memoir

Library of Congress Control Number 2003115383
ISBN 9747949-0-2 (Paperback)

Acknowledgments

I AM GRATEFUL TO:

My husband, Jerry, who patiently put up with all the time I spent in my Word Shop to produce this book and asked so many times, "Is it done yet?" My high school French teacher, Sister Mary Marcelle, S.S.A., who planted the seed that germinated and grew to fruition sixty years later.

A story I wrote, *My Little Brother,* (fiction) caused Sister to comment, "You could write a book someday." Yah, right. I took it lightly then, but over time as I got more interested in writing, her words kept resurfacing, and in 1999 my first book, *Worcester's Union Station: The Monument and the Memories,* was accepted and published second time out by Ambassador Books, Inc., of Worcester. Now, I am at it again writing book number two, with yet another book of stories, poems, and anecdotes in the wings.

Mrs. Claire Cotter, English teacher, also planted a seed that grew to fruition. If it were not for her suggesting that I go to college, I never would have thought I was capable of doing so.

Richard Belair, Creative Writing teacher at Assumption College. The wealth of knowledge I gleaned from his suggestions and great ideas for changes in my essays and stories, helped me immensely. My daughter Denise Hobby, whose final editing, great patience and helpful suggestions, contributed to the success of this book.

★ ★ ★ ★ ★ ★ ★

Foreword

As a child I was pitifully shy, to the point where I would hide in a closet when company came. My grade school years left me with low self-esteem because I was always at the tail end of my class. On rare occasions I was delighted when I came in fourth of fifth to the last. But the most degrading experience of all was that I repeated the fourth and sixth grades. What made matters worse is that no one in my family of ten brothers and sisters had ever repeated a grade. By the time I reached seventh grade I had had it with being teased by the smart kids about being held back. I retaliated by saying, "I'm smarter than you are, I learned everything twice!"

The one thing that kept me from being a total failure is that I had a natural ability to write. The nuns at Holy Name of Jesus School could not understand how I could write so well when I did not know beans about grammar rules. When I was promoted to eighth grade I had doubts that I would ever graduate from grammar school. I struggled all year hoping I would not embarrass my parents by having to repeat the eighth grade. Phew! I just barely made it. I graduated *Avec Succès* just a cut above *Certificate*.

High school! How was I ever going to manage that?

The Superior at Holy Name advised my mother not to send me to Holy Family High. It would be too difficult for me. Girl's Trade would be better for me where I could learn to cook and sew. Cook and sew? Yuck!

My mother, a devout Catholic, had no intention of sending me to a public school. In those days Catholics were *duty bound* to send their children to parochial schools. My mother told the Superior, "If you will not accept her I am going to see Father Tessier."

To avoid a confrontation with the Pastor the Superior enrolled me at Holy Family High, but only *on trial*. Luckily, I did well in most subjects. I enjoyed typing, shorthand, English literature, French literature, and religion. I barely made it out of high school and again at the tail end of my class.

There were only six students in the class – all girls. To my embarrassment the inscriptions on our diplomas were announced to the audience. Two of the graduates had Très Grande Distinction, two had Grande Distinction, one had Distinction, and I had Satisfaction.

Besides the great titles on their diplomas they all received gifts for special achievements except me. I did not begrudge their success – they earned it – but I was crushed because I did not receive an award for French Composition or the Religion Award because that is where my strengths were. Unfortunately, students had to have passing grades in all subjects to qualify for an award. I failed bookkeeping, business English, and French grammar. Nevertheless, I have pleasant memories of being chosen Cheftaine de L'équippe Missionaire. I collected pennies for missionaries abroad. I made tableaus of missionary scenes in a cupboard in religion class. One in particular comes to mind. It was an Eskimo village in Alaska with fake snow and paper igloos. I used white tissue paper, cotton balls, and glittery mica to make it look realistic. A cardboard cut-out of a missionary holding a cross dominated the scene.

Back to graduation night. My mother, sensing my disappointment at not receiving an award said, "The writing on your diploma does not matter, I'm proud that you have a high school education."

After graduation I sent for how-to books on achieving success. Dale Carnegie's two books, *How to Win Friends and Influence People,* and *How to Stop Worrying and Start Living,* were my constant companions. I read those two books dog-eared. I identified with Carnegie because like me, he was shy too. But he worked his way out of his timidity and all his other problems that held him back. As Carnegie advised I reviewed his book each month. I applied his principles at every opportunity. It was not easy for me to come out of my shell, but I worked at it long and hard and I succeeded.

In 1945 I married Gerard Arsenault. We had five children. During their growing up years I read all the books on success I could find and I applied their teachings. Twenty years into our marriage I came upon Norman Vincent Peale's, *The Power of Positive Thinking.* It was the catalyst that changed the rest of my life. Peale gave me the confidence and the courage I needed to take charge of my life and to not be afraid to take risks. I took correspondence courses in writing, painting, photo restoration, and many other courses.

In my spare time I did freelance writing and became a published author of articles, essays, poetry, and anecdotes. Although I enjoyed freelancing I wanted to try something new. I looked into a nursing career. Then came an obstacle in my path. In order to get into the nursing school I needed my high school transcript which I destroyed after graduation, because I was embarrassed at the inscription, *Satisfaction.* I called the school department. All the transcripts for 1942 were lost. The old nuns had gone to their *just reward* so there was no proof that I graduated from high school. There must be a way, I thought. There has got to be a way. I decided to take the High School Equivalency Test (GED). When I told the teacher I had graduated from high school, she said I could not apply for the program because I had already been through high school, but when I told her that the *high school* I graduated from was a two-year Commercial Course and not a four-year high school, she allowed me to take the GED test.

To my surprise I passed all the tests and placed in the 93 percentile nationwide in English. My English teacher Claire Cotter, told me I should consider going to college. I was stunned. I did not think I was smart enough. By then the idea of becoming a nurse no longer interested me, but the idea of getting a college degree, did. However, I put that idea on hold because I did not feel ready. I began to look for ways to pass my time besides pecking pretty prose, poems and anecdotes on my Royal typewriter. I searched the Want Ads for a job. Experienced only need apply, the ads read. The most experience I had was as an office clerk at Norton Company and as a lady welder, linking anchor chains for the navy during World War Two. The good jobs required degrees. Well, I didn't have an A.A, a B.A, an M.A, or a PhD, so I decided it was time to go and get a couple of those.

The empty nest was upon us. At age 55 I enrolled as a full-time day student at Quinsigamond Community College in Worcester, Massachusetts. I signed up for five courses. How daring could I get? Reality soon set in and I withdrew from Math and Western Civilization. Second semester I made the Dean's List. My self-esteem grew by leaps and bounds. **I WAS NOT AT THE TAIL END OF MY CLASS ANYMORE!** In the third semester I became editor of the college newspaper, *The Open Door.* I graduated with High Honors in 1982, made Who's Who in Junior Colleges, and received a plaque inscribed:

IN RECOGNITION OF YOUR OUTSTANDING CONTRIBUTIONS AS EDITOR OF THE QUINSIGAMOND COLLEGE NEWSPAPER

In 1983 I attended Worcester State College for one semester where I took courses in Literature, Journalism, and Tutoring Writing. I then transferred to Assumption College in 1984, and earned a B.A. degree in Liberal Studies. I graduated cum laude at age 66 in 1991.

"What you can do or dream you can begin it. Boldness has genius, power, and magic in it."

—Goethe

★ ★ ★ ★ ★ ★ ★

CONTENTS

PART I
Breaking Loose

In the Beginning
French I and II
Audio-Tutorial Biology
Drawing I
Photography I & II
English Comp I
Literature I
Practicum in Community Experience

PART II
Mind Bogglers

Western Civilization
Mathematics I & II
Statistics
Metrics
Intro to Psychology
Personal Growth

PART III

Etcetera

Potpouri

★ ★ ★ ★ ★ ★ ★

PART I

BREAKING LOOSE

IN THE BEGINNING

In 1979, when I signed up as a full-time day student at Quinsigamond Community College, I took French for an easy *A* and Biology for an easy *F*. I announced to my family I was going to college to broaden my horizons. They were astonished! They got over it. No doubt they thought I was cracking up from the strain of having five kids. An earful of negative comments followed:

"But Ma, you're fifty-five-years old."

"You're too old for school."

"What'll our friends think?"

"It's dangerous out there Ma, druggies and weirdo's you know."

One of the kids remained speechless, but my husband, totally abashed asked plaintively,

"Will you be home for supper?"

"Forcrineoutloud!" I yelled. "It's not the end of the world. I'm going to college to accumulate knowledge. Not to worry. I'm not going to smoke pot or go to beer parties."

I assured my husband I would be home for supper and that nothing was going to change. One week into the semester I had added the following words to my vocabulary: Right on, Piece of cake, Wing it, Whatever turns you on, You got it, and Hang in there kid. When I told my husband I volunteered as a reporter for *The Open Door* newspaper I could read his mind ... Next thing I'll know she'll be president of the college .... At the end of the first semester I was invited to Spree Day. I accepted. Of course I did not go at risk of being committed to the funny farm by my family.

During the fifties and sixties my kids were saying, "I want to be me." Little did they know all the while I was thinking I wanted to be me too, but when? After all those years of changing diapers - the Birdseye cloth kind - sterilizing bottles, making formulas from scratch; spending sleepless nights rocking the babies; putting up with the terrible two's five times; scrubbing the kitchen floor on my hands and knees; baking bread; and besides all that, chauffeuring the kids all over town just to keep up with the Joneses's kids. Can you blame me for longing to get on with my life?

I wanted desperately to do something intellectual. I thirsted for knowledge. I yearned to hone my writing skills. I was eager to read the classics and be able to say with an air of savoir faire, "Elementary my dear Watson," and know what the source was.

Now, at last, I no longer thought I wanted to be me, I was me. After I became me I could hardly wait to begin my new adventure. I was nervous. Was I doing the right thing? I refused to let my true feelings show. I walked tall on campus, hugging my books; pretending I was nineteen, when I was probably older than all the professors. At the onset of my college days I met only one other student over 50, but by the time I graduated in 1982 a few more had trickled in. I could have finished in 1981, but I wanted to stay for another semester to run the newspaper one more time. I kept *Statistics* for last. I knew it was a tough course and not my favorite subject.

The young students made quite an impression on me. It was invigorating to be in their midst. They were so new and fresh, with great ambitions and interesting ideas. I learned from them by observing their behavior. They knew better than to speak out in class the way I did, but keeping my thoughts to myself was hard for me to do. More than once I blurted my thoughts out at inopportune moments and embarrassed myself to death. Would you believe I asked one professor what all those little red check marks next to my errors were in front of the whole class? Another time I asked a professor what that little dash next to my *A* meant. What a nerve! I knew very well what it meant. I was just miffed that he didn't give me a straight *A*. He probably wanted to take me down a peg for being a wise mouth. I am surprised he did not give me an *F* on the next test for embarrassing him. If I continued such behavior I would probably be the first grandmother to get kicked out of college. I was getting spoiled by my *A's* and I wanted more. One day I felt like such a fool after speaking out in class. I was so upset I wanted to quit college, but I swallowed my pride and continued on.

I reminded myself every day that you do not argue with the professor, or put him/her on the spot. So what if your biology professor believes the world began with a big bang and you believe God made the world in six days and on the seventh day He rested. You have to remember, the professor is the teacher and you are the student even if he looks younger than your own kids. But, do you know how hard it is to keep silent after you have been teacher/boss to your kids all those years, and suddenly you are the kid and you must respect the teacher? Not an easy transition of roles.

The professors, in general, were eager to share their knowledge with me, but a few of them seemed intimidated by my presence, and that made me uneasy. I must have appeared mature and full of wisdom. Little did they know I was shaking in my boots in their presence, that I was a struggler in school, and that I graduated from grammar and high school at the tail end of my class.

Going to college broadened my horizons all right. I learned in biology class that all men and women are *really* created equal. Honest. My biology professor said so himself. Did you know that when a baby is conceived 23 chromosomes from the male and 23 chromosomes from the female become part of the new life? Sounds pretty equal to me. Speaking of equality, one day I told my husband from now on we're having turns cooking supper. Know what he said?

"From now on we're going to McDonald's every other night."

My husband and kids knew that when I set my mind to do something I would see it through no matter what. Their reaction to my decision to go to college did not sway me one bit. I was on a mission and I looked forward to my new adventure with great excitement.

Because I grew up in a French household, I was confident that *French I & II* would be easy.

****

FRENCH I & II

GROWING UP OUR FAMILY SPOKE French in the house and English outdoors. Our French/Canadian/Acadian heritage affected a curious blend of expressions understood only by family and French acquaintances, but not by the nuns at Holy Family High. French Canuck, a mix of French Canadian peppered with pure slang was our daily fare, and it sometimes got me into trouble in high school French class. Speaking two languages was an advantage, but speaking Canuck had its drawbacks.

One day, Sister Mary Marcelle sent me to the board to choose the correct answer between two sentences she had written down. Chalk in hand, palms sweaty, I hesitated for several moments and tried to figure out the correct answer.

Sister quipped impatiently, "Well, what's the answer?"

"Bain," I mumbled, "C'èst ça aubedon ça."

Meaning it is either this or that. I did not know the answer so I figured that was the next best thing to saying nothing. I was mortified when Sister said, "Va t'assoir aubedon."

Meaning "Go sit down, aubedon." The class roared with laughter. When I got home I looked up aubedon in the dictionary. It was not there. My father thought the whole thing was hilarious and he told the story at every family gathering.

Before I took French in college, I dug out my French grammar books to review. I committed all the grammar rules and conjugations to memory. I breezed through *French I & II.*

Even though I hardly studied, I ended up with an *A* minus.

According to some students, *Audio-Tutorial Biology* was a tough two-semester course. I braced myself and said a few prayers, hoping I would at least get a passing mark.

****

AUDIO-TUTORIAL BIOLOGY

I BAWLED AT LEAST THREE times a week in biology class. The course consisted of listening to cassette tapes and doing readings on my own. Friday of each week was test day. That course had my eyes bugging out of my head, such was the voluminous amount of reading I had to do. My reason for not taking general biology is that I was squeamish about dissecting a frog. I would have quit college first. I didn't have the guts to clean a fish never mind cut up a frog. Once, when my husband brought home a horn-pout, I had nightmares about its ugly face with stiff whiskers and beady black eyes. He got rid of the fish because he knew I would not eat it even if he cooked it himself. He thinks I am weird because I will not kill a fly, an ant, or a spider. He steps on anything that moves and swats anything that flies. My theory is, they are all God's creatures and they must be here for a reason.

I was pretty shook up when I had to draw my own blood to check my blood type. I had to stab my middle finger with a lancet. I hesitated. It took me fifteen minutes to finally make the incision. I did it because the professor said I would not pass the course unless I did the assignment. He had no mercy. My sad green eyes and pleading expression did not sway him one bit.

One day the professor, who had a thing about jungle weeds, started to water the plants that hung over the learning cubicles with a two-gallon galvanized bucket. S-P-L-A-S-H! I was jolted out of my stupor from the cold niagara that washed off my mascara and threw my glasses off-course. My screech scared the professor right off the chair and he mumbled apologetically, "Oh, uh, s'cuse me, uh, I thought you were one of the plants." That goes to show you how long I had been there growing moss out of my wig. I wanted to hit him with *The Pros and Cons of Psychosurgery,* but instead, I left, absolutely frustrated, disgusted and mad, if it is possible to experience three emotions at once.

As much as I suffered misery, agony, and pain all during the course, I left with a wealth of knowledge about issues that I was only vaguely aware of before. What did I know about the DNA, the double helix, amniocentesis, or in-vitro fertilization? I know I will never be a candidate for the latter, but at least I know what it is all about. I heaved a sigh of relief when the two semesters were over. I just barely passed the course. Nevertheless, I will never forget the 4.0 mark I received for my project, *The Pros and Cons of Psychosurgery,* with a written comment from the professor: Excellent! Well done!

I needed a rest from all that brain work so I signed up for *Drawing I* next semester.

****

DRAWING I

ART WAS MY FAVORITE SUBJECT in grammar school so I thought *Drawing I* would be a breeze. What could be hard about drawing? Surprise. In the first class I did a double-take at the display on the table where the professor had placed a large maple tree branch that had leaves and twigs of various sizes. I had just begun to draw the leaves when the professor announced that he wanted us to draw the spaces between the leaves. The s-p-a-c-e-s? Well, the professor seemed perfectly sane, so I attempted to draw the spaces. It was the hardest thing I had ever done.

The next assignment was a ladder-back chair, again drawing only the spaces. That was a little easier because it involved straight lines as opposed to the intricate shapes of the maple tree spaces. I was so taken with space drawing that one day I drew the spaces between the double fluorescent lights in the kitchen, the spaces between the tines of a fork and the handle of the coffee pot. My husband was watching but said nothing, until I knelt down to draw the spaces between the grid on the bottom of the fridge. He said, "Please tell me you're not going to college to learn whatever that is you're doing." I ignored him.

Actually, my drawing improved considerably as a result of my obsession with the space drawing technique. I noted that when I focused on the spaces between the object rather than on the object itself, I was actually outlining the object. All during the course I kept observing spaces at risk of being carried away by men in white coats. The technique was responsible for my getting honked at from cars behind me when I stopped at a red light. More and more I found myself observing the areas above traffic lights. I marvelled at all the spaces between the electric wires that criss-cross at intersections. Many times I would be looking up instead of watching for the light to turn green, while the driver in back of me honked the horn for me to get going.

Drawing I opened up a whole new area of perception. I am convinced it helped me with the composition of scenes in the photography course I took the following semester.

★★★★★★★

PHOTOGRAPHY I & II

My first camera was a Kodak Instamatic. It served me well for many years. After the kids were grown and gone my interest in photography grew, and I bought a Nikkormat F/T2. It served me well also. *Photography I* involved lectures and class assignments, but since I had my own dark room I developed and printed photos at home. I did not like working in the basement however, because of the eerie atmosphere created by the amber safe lights and the real or imaginary noises I heard. I was especially spooked one night when I enlarged a wedding photo of my paternal grandparents, long since dead. When I put the exposed paper in the developer tray, I heard footsteps on the cellar stairs. Developing time - two minutes - had come to an end. A knock on the door caused me to drop the print face down on the floor before I had a chance to put it in the stop-bath tray. Disaster. I suspected my ancestors did not want me fooling around with their images. The door creaked open. My husband said, "It's two o'clock. I thought you got asphyxiated by the fumes."

The following semester I took *Photography II* on Independent Study. Never again. You talk about boring. Even though I had some contact with the professor I felt marooned. It turned out to be harder than attending classes. I did the housework hit-and-miss and the cooking via can opener. I would constantly bug my husband about my prints. "What do you think? Should I keep the one with the dark background or this one or that one?" By the end of the semester he felt like he deserved three credits too.

One winter afternoon my husband and I roamed the seven hills of Worcester and beyond. We drove to the nearby town of Rutland to shoot photos of barns. I just could not pass up two cows in a snow-filled meadow. As I approached the pastoral scene, WOOSH! I sank knee-deep in the snow. I held the camera above my head for fear I would get the lens wet, while my husband stood next to the car laughing and making no attempt to rescue me. When the cows went M-O-O! I froze. I visualized the morning headlines: WORCESTER WOMAN TRAMPLED TO DEATH BY TWO COWS IN RUTLAND. Finally, I managed a shot. My husband, still laughing, came to drag me out as the cows started to walk toward me. So much for pastoral scenes.

I learned some valuable techniques in *Photography I & II,* but it took me a while to get used to the amber lights and eerie noises in the basement. Eager to get back to classes and socializing with the students, I took *English Comp I* the following semester.

****

ENGLISH COMP I

When I signed up for college, I had been a published writer for several years and I had a fairly good handle on the English language. But, many years had passed since high school graduation so I decided to take *English Comp I* to brush up on the subject. I cannot tell a lie. I was bored out of my gourd, so on the pretense of taking notes I composed poetry, wrote Scripture passages, decided what to cook for supper, or made shopping lists. When I ran out of ideas I drew cartoons.

One day as I took a break from my fake notes and stared at the handsome professor, POP! A STORY IDEA! ... She was in love with her English professor, who was young enough to be her son .... Imagine that! Believe me, I had no designs on the young man whatsoever. That is just how my writer's imagination works. And that is as far as that *flash of brilliance* has gotten.

On one of our essays the professor wanted something original. I was positive no one else would come up with *The Ups and Downs of Wearing False Teeth*. When the professor returned the papers he said he lost mine.

Since he was going to have the students read their essays in class, he no doubt was shocked when I noted that I would gladly read my essay without my false teeth. I thought it would make an impression on young students who did not brush regularly. Luckily, I am a fanatic about making copies. Because I did not get to read my essay in class, I am using it here for all the world to see.

The Ups and Downs of Wearing False Teeth

One of the best things about wearing false teeth is that you can take them or leave them. Who says you have to wear them all the time? So if you do not mind looking like a clone of Popeye, go right ahead. My friend Freda and I have it made. At eating functions we go to the rest room after a meal to rinse our teeth. Once, the attendant peeked under the door wondering what we were doing in the disabled stall so long. We were washing the sink with liquid peppermint hand soap to make sure everything went down the drain.

A male relative of mine carries his false teeth in his shirt pocket in case he meets up with the Pope or the President of the United States. He just cannot get used to wearing those *damn things.* The last wedding we attended he went toothless and swore he would never do it again. While trying to sip champagne for the toast, the bubbly cascaded down his shirt, tie, and down his trousers. He was so shook up he ran to the rest room to dry his clothes from the heat of the hand dryer.

Another good thing about wearing false teeth is that you are free from the dentist and that dreaded chair, until your gums start to recede, that is. That's when people on the phone ask if you are chewing gum drops.

And when your top teeth fall down in public it is a clear sign that Poli-Grip does not work anymore. The *Upside* of wearing false teeth is that you never have a toothache. The *Downside* is that you can't chew regular gum because it sticks to the palate, eating corn on the cob is embarrassing when your teeth stay on the cob, and when you sleep over someone's house you keep your teeth in your mouth and not in a jar in the bathroom to gross out your hosts.

****

OUR NEXT ASSIGNMENT was a descriptive essay. I wrote about playing a game of Scrabble at my German dauthter-in-law's house.

SH-CRABBLE

ERIKA LEARNED THE English language fairly quickly when our son brought her to the States during the sixties, but she still had trouble letting go of the Sh's with words beginning with S. I figured that playing Scrabble on a weekly basis would help her get rid of the Sh's. It did not.

"Are you cummin' over for Sh-Crabble today?" She would ask.

My answer was always in the affirmative. Every Thursday my dark green 1973 scratched-up Malibu took me to her house to *peacefully* play Scrabble, hoping that little John, my grandson would be busy playing outside.

One morning as I drove up the dirt driveway that led to the black-shuttered, gold-toned Cape, the crunch of tires on the driveway snapping, crackling, and popping, reminded me that I forgot to eat my bowl of Rice Krispies, such was my insane preoccupation with Scrabble. I admit that I am a word nut who would rather play Scrabble than eat. I was hardly out of the car when John wrapped himself around me with the fervor of a chimpanzee. My brown-rimmed plastic bifocals flew off my nose and landed lens down in a sea of assorted field stones. John held his hand out for the Cracker Jacks I always brought. I fished in my brown crocheted satchel, cluttered with assorted stuff: A deck of Red Bicycle playing cards, a bunch of dull-looking keys on a black shoestring, a dog-eared copy *Strunk & White's Elements of Style,* and other satchel stuff. The Cracker Jacks were underneath the meleé. As John grabbed the Cracker Jacks out of my hand he ran toward the front door where Erika waited. His blonde John-John haircut flipped up and down as he ran. I pondered ... John, child of my child, I wondered if he liked me for me or the Cracker Jacks ....

Erika, trying hard to sound Americanized greeted me with, "Hi dare!"

Hummel figurines adorned her cozy warm kitchen. The smell of freshly brewed coffee and spicy apple strudel filled the room. After our snack we started the game.

"You have the lowest letter," I said, "it's your move."

We hardly put the words *man* and *penny* on the board when John came in howling and holding his bloody knee.

"Wha-a-a-h, Ow-ow-ow, Ma it hurts. Wha-a-a-h."

Good grief, don't tell me it's going to be one of those days, I thought. Erika tended to John's knee. About five minutes went by and John came in again.

"Get dat verm outa hier, don't you know dat ist cherms!" Erika yelled.

I began to have second thoughts about finishing the game.

I just hope he stays out of our hair for the rest of the day. After a while Erika checked on John because he had a habit of straying.

"Chon, get outa da shtreet or yoo vil get hit by da car."

"But Ma, I'm lookin' for my toad. He got outa da can las' night. I have to feed him some bugs or he's gonna die."

"Gettover hier und gettin' da haüs or I vil tel yoo fadder! Dat kit is maykin' me krayzee." Erika complained, as she led John in front of the TV to watch Mr. Rogers.

"For dat he keeps k-viet tanks to Got."

Back to Scrabble. We no sooner resumed the game when John yelled, "Ma, there's something wrong with the TV."

"Vel, fichs it." Erika said.

"No, you fix it. You know what Dad said about me touching the knobs."

After Erika fixed the TV she said, "I can't vait 'til nex yier ven Chon goes to kinta-gatten, den vee can play Sh-Crabble in peace."

The game was over. "See you nex veek, Ja?"

I agreed, but I really felt like saying, "See you next year!"

****

IN MY THIRD semester I became editor of the college newspaper, *The Open Door.* After awhile I wondered why students did not submit articles for publication. After asking around, a popular excuse was that the students had difficulty with punctuations, especially the semicolon. They complained that they did not know when to use it.

"Then don't use it." I advised.

In the next issue of the paper I boldly aired my views about the semicolon and that I would like to do away with it once and for all. Truly, is there anyone out there who would come right out and say how they r-e-a-l-l-y feel about the semicolon? As far as I know this is a *first.* Why should a reader have to disrupt his/her train of thought for the sake of a lousy semicolon to show him/her they are supposed to pause here. They know when to pause here. Common sense tells them what is going on. That advice did not sit right with a professor in the English Department who wrote a rebuttal in the next issue.

Dear Editor,

In the last issue of *The Open Door,* you ran an article that tramples the poor old semicolon. However, before everyone stomps it to death, we should remember that the semicolon is a signal, an asset in the written language. Many of us see the signal; nevertheless, we fail to note its function. Why? We do not notice the major break between the main clause; we are, in fact, insensitive to the weight assigned to facts and issues. Another function of the semicolon is to eliminate the confusion resulting from running together items that belong in separate categories.

1. Please mail your requests to the following cities: Worcester, Massachusetts; Arid, Arizona; Panacea, Florida; and Placebo, California.

2. Everybody should bring the following items: slippers, shoes, and overshoes; dress shirts, at least three; athletic supports - including jockstraps, bras, and cheerleaders magazines - *Playboy, Playgirl, and PlayGay;* how-to books - such as *Wiring Made Easy: A Shocking Experience* and *Luxury Plumbing: The Royal Flush;* and advice books - such as *Freelance Writing: Going for Broke* and *Creative Teaching: Risking Absurdity.* Therefore, if we were to do away with the semicolon, we would be destroying a signaling device that can add emphasis, energy, pause, clarity, and cohesiveness to our written communication. —English Department.

Next issue: Dear Professor, A thousand pardons.

Please forgive my insensitivity towards the semicolon. I always shyed away from using it because, like the students, I did not know when to use it either. Thank you so much for explaining the rules.

—The Editor

Literature I was next on my agenda.

****

LITERATURE I

BEFORE I SIGNED UP FOR Literature, I thought the course would consist of writing essays and doing book reports, but as I read the syllabus I found out I would have to analyze poetry. Oh, no! I scanned the textbook. What in the world does ab, ab, have to do with anything? Then when I came upon such words as metonymy, synechdoche, onomatopoia, and other never heard of five-dollar words, I thought, there goes my poor brain. I was never exposed to such terms in high school. Now I have to put up with this! I could hardly pronounce the words let alone know what they meant. Sheesh! The only way I could remember all those definitions was to repeat them over and over during all my waking hours.

The poems I had difficulty with were the ones that did not make any sense to me at all at first, second, and third readings. Someone said it is like looking at an abstract painting. It depends on how it affects you personally at the time. Well, personally, those poems did not affect me at all. Check W. H. Alden's, *As I Walked Out One Evening* and see what you make of it.

> "The glacier knocks in the cupboard
> The desert sighs in the bed
> And the crack in the teacup opens
> A lane to the land of the dead."

W-H-A-T! Luckily, I did not have to analyze that poem. I guess if you like that kind of poetry it is all right with me. I always lean towards the easy to read poets like William Wordsworth, who believed that "the finest poetry could be written in the simplest words."

I am with you, William. My favorite of his is *Daffodils.* I know it by heart. It is so fluid, so beautiful, that it lifts my mood whenever I recite it aloud when I am home alone.

The mere thickness of *Anthology of American Literature,* (1,915 pages) almost scared me right out of the college book store. Yikes! In high school *Prose and Poetry* was miniscule by comparison. Curious, I leafed through the anthology before classes began. In my teens I was not fond of reading entire books. It was an effort to finish George Elliot's *Silas Marner.* For those who do not know it the author's real name is Mary Ann Evans. In those days most women authors had to use men's names as their by-line. How would those men feel if the shoe was on the other foot and they had to use women's names, huh?

I was delighted to read on page 254 that Tom Paine spoke out for the rights of men (and of women). Hey! Why is (and of women) in parenthesis pray tell? Could it be a metaphor for women being *fenced in?* Further on I was pleased to read how Anne Bradstreet felt about women's rights. "She was one of the first women in America to speak on her own behalf." In her poem, *The Prologue,* (page 94) Bradstreet writes:

"I am obnoxious to each carping tongue
" Who says my hand a needle better fits."

I find it unfair that out of 1,915 pages of text, only three female authors were featured compared to forty-two of the male gender. You mean to tell me the only female authors worthy of note in the 1600's were Anne Bradstreet, Mary Rowlandson, and Phyllis Wheatley? Sounds kind of biased to me. To top it all off "Bradstreet's first collection of poems had no identifiable by-line. Her writings merely read: by a Gentlewoman of Those Parts." You talk about *unequal rights.* Upon further research I discovered that the Puritan mentality of the times frowned on writing as an unseemly behavior for women.

I wonder how many talented women went unnoticed because of such attitudes. Shame on those responsible for this. I am grateful to the brave women who wrote in spite of the negative attitudes of men who thought they were the only ones fit to be writers. Thank God for the courageous women of that time who spoke for the rights of women. If it were not for them I would not be sitting here at my iMac computer putting my thoughts on paper, being published, and getting paid for it to boot. Thank you foremothers.

I learned all about my city fathers in the next course.

****

PRACTICUM IN COMMUNITY EXPERIENCE

I CHOSE *PRACTICUM* BECAUSE I was curious about what my city fathers were up to at those weekly meetings. After the first class I became totally involved with the course and I loved it.

First meeting:

I was flabbergasted by the appearance of my city fathers. Two of them looked as though they were not going to make it to their chairs. Luckily, they sat down through the meeting because I do not think they could have stood up for more than five minutes without fainting. I was doubly flabbersgasted by all the hoopla that went into the proposed changes at the site of a street light. After the three-hour meeting I went home exhausted.

Second meeting:

I decided to put an item on the agenda. No forms available. I went home mad because I did not get anything accomplished. The next day I went back to the *hall* and I was given the old City Hall runaround. I asked where I could get an agenda form. The person at the first desk told me to go upstairs. The person upstairs told me to go downstairs.

The person downstairs told me to go to the basement. By that time I was ready to hang it all up and forget about putting an item on the agenda, but after getting my second wind I marched straight to the manager's office to ask him if this was any way to run a *hall.* He was not there. I asked his secretary where I could get an agenda form and she directed me to the proper office.

Back to the manager's office. I asked the secretary where I could get a copy of the *Town Report* from which I planned to do my research. She informed me that I had come to the right place. I was willing to pay any reasonable price, such was my total interest in the course, but I was stunned when she quoted a price of ten dollars. While fishing nervously in my brown drawstring satchel for an envelope labeled *Food,* I wondered if I had enough one-dollar bills. I had only nine. When I started to count four quarters from a Kodak film container the secretary said, "Here, I'll give it to you for nothing. I don't usually do this you know. Just don't tell anyone, please."

I rushed home to devour the book. Believe me, if I had paid ten dollars for that book, I never would have uttered another clean word. Dullsville? Who cares about the date, the place, and the hour the Cemetery Commissioners had a banquet and a good time was had by all, or about the City Settlement marker that needed a comma removed for grammatical reasons, and a crew of three foremen, three supervisors to watch the foremen, and three policemen to direct traffic, all for the purpose of removing a COMMA? Good grief, Mr. Manager!

Third meeting:

I decided to put the Dog Leash Law on the agenda because that issue hit home. There was no such law in the city but a dog-restraining order was on the books, which meant that owners must keep their dogs on their property at all times. Oh, really. Then what are all those creatures that run up and down my street all night long? Big cats that bark?

By now I knew the *hall* like the back of my mittens. Finally, it was over.

With my last bit of information recorded, I dragged my tired torso to the parking lot behind the library and guess what was on my windshield? A ticket! I was just an *nth* of a second over on the parking meter. G-r-r-! I wanted to spit at City Hall, but it was beyond my spitting range.

I experienced many frustrations at City Hall, nevertheless, *Practicum in Community Experience* turned out to be a great learning tool for me. It forced me to go to public places I had never been to before, and to set up interviews with city officials. The latter gave me the self-confidence I needed to deal with the public. Not only did I learn about my city fathers, but I also learned about putting an item on the agenda, the dog leash Law; perk tests; building codes; school departments, and town versus city government. All subjects I never would have known about cooped up in the house. Just one bit of advice should you take such a course. Do not hang around City Hall too long. You might get a ticket as I did, or crack up under the strain.

The foregoing courses were mild compared to what lay ahead.

****

PART II

MIND BOGGLERS

WESTERN CIVILIZATION

IN MY *WESTERN CIVILIZATION* COURSE, I was absolutely positive the professor was hung on Rome, so I memorized Italy's boot until I knew it better than my own shoe. Would you believe there was not one question about the boot on the first test? I began to say Hail Mary's aloud. The whole test was about the Great Wall of China. Well, I did not think the wall was so great so I did not study anything about it. I wrote a note to the professor: Confucious say, "He who talks about Italy every day should have some questions about Italy on tests!"

The professor was big on numbers. Did it matter to me that "no less than 19 Emperors reigned during the calamitous half-century between 236 and 285 during the third century? Or that during the reign of Marcus Aurelius (161-180) the Empire had been struck by a devastating plague, or that between A.D. 256 and 280 the cost of living rose 1000 per cent?"

Now I know what my kids went through. They could not figure out why in the world they had to study algebra. What were they going to use it for in real life they would ask. I beg the same question about western civilization.

On the next test the professor threw the book at us. We were asked to name important dates during the Roman Republic. How kind of the professor to give us a hint. All the dates were B.C., and all we had to do was fill in the blanks. Plus, we had to fill the little blue book with an essay about what the professor lectured on the previous week. Huh? I did not remember what he said that morning never mind what he said last week. I tried to fudge my way through the blue book but the professor saw right through me.

I failed the test. Lucky for me the professor, sensing my chagrin, allowed me to take the test again. I got 65 for a grade and I passed the course with a C minus, which did a number on my grade point average. I decided from then on not to second-guess what was going to be on tests and simply follow the syllabus.

Little did I know there was something much worse than *Western Civilization* just around the corner.

****

MATHEMATICS I & II

SINCE MATH WAS MY WORST subject in school, I decided to get that course out of the way as soon as possible. Little did my professor know that long divisions and fractions blew my mind, and algebra, which was suposed to help me develop reasoning power, only helped to confuse me all the more. Mathematics, a required subject in my Liberal Arts course nearly had me do an about face straight home to *The Young and the Restless,* but I decided to hang in there and struggle along.

When the professor handed me my first test marked with a big red *F* I was crushed. I told the professor I wanted to drop the course. She advised me to go home and study the book and I could take the test over the next day. I studied until the wee hours. It took me a long time to figure out the sequences Fibonnaci was trying to put across. I finally got off of page one. Now, I had the Fibonnaci sequences firmly rooted in my head and along came a French mathematician named Edouard Anatole Lucas on page two who introduced his sequences with a two instead of a one as Fibonnaci did. Why couldn't he leave well enough alone?

I skipped page two and went on to other things, hoping the Lucas sequences would not be on the test. They were. Page three revealed that "Blaise Pascal's triangle was introduced to the world in 1665, but the triangle had appeared more than two-hundred years earlier in publications by the Chinese mathematicians, Yan Yui and Chu shih-Chieh." I wish those geniuses had kept those things to themselves.

On rare occasions I came across something easy like the Data Processing Card on page seven. At least all was not lost. I skipped pages eight and nine because they were mind-boggling. I was not about to start figuring distances according to Bode's Law for the relative distances of planets from the sun. For example, check the following brain teaser:

"If Mercury is ignored and Venus is considered the first planet, then the bode distance (call it B) can be computed from the planet's position p (for Venus p equals o, for earth p equals 1, etc.) by the formula, B equals 3.2p plus 4. Verify the formula for Venus, Mars, the asteroids, and Saturn. (Note that 2 degrees equals 1)."

Can you blame me for skipping pages eight and nine? Thereafter, I skipped all the pages I did not understand which brought me to page thirty-eight and The Magic Squares. It was easy. Yay! I was so happy I found something I understood that I did the Magic Square problem over and over again just for fun.

So far, I understood three things, the Fibonnaci Sequences, the Data Processing Card, and the Magic Squares. As I flipped the pages I came upon rubber sheet geometry. I noted that the Frenchman who founded that branch of mathematics (Topology) was Henri Poincare. I was devastated!

I withdrew from the course. POINCARE, translated to English means POINTY SQUARE! With a name like that I just knew that course would drive me right out of my mind. I took the course later on when my load was not so heavy.

With the help of a math tutor and a lot of determination I passed the course with a B plus! I thought I was through with math, but in order to graduate, another math course was required. Read on and suffer along with me through *Statistics.*

****

STATISTICS

Absolutely nothing prepared me for a college Statistics course. In my youth all eighth-grade parochial school students were advised to go to parochial high schools and take commercial courses. In grammar school in the forties algebra was not on the curriculum, so I knew nothing about those funny little sideways M's, and little x's mixed with other weird designs that look like fly legs divided by N. At Holy Family High we learned Typing, Shorthand, Bookkeeping, Business English, French Grammar, French and English Literature and Religion .

So before I took *Statistics* I decided to bone up on the subject because I heard nothing but horror stories about Stats. I found a Statistic textbook in a pile of books at a flea market for twenty-five cents. See where they end up? Three things impressed me as I leafed through its pages.

This Statististic book is not for math majors. They can't figure it out either.

You will need a knowledge of basic algebra to get by. Get by? I hope I can get started.

Recollections from basic algebra. How can I recall something I did not learn?

I now challenge any male Statistics professor to decipher the following instructions for a Granny Square, providing of course the professor has not had any previous crocheting experience

Starting at ctr. C5. Join w sl st to form rng. C3, (counts as 1 dc) 2 dc in rng. C2, dc in rng.

C2, 3 dc in rng, C2, 3 dc in rng. C2, Join w sl st to tp of C3.

Now, suppose I am the professor and you, Mr. Professor, are the student. I have written the above instructions on the board and I say,

"As you will recall from basic crocheting ..."

Frustrating? Mind-boggling? You bet.

"Why can't you decipher this? Have you forgotten?"

Of course you haven't forgotten. You never learned it. See what I mean?

The worst experience of all in Statistics class was watching all the other students nodding yesses that they understood the linear correlation coefficient measure of strength of linear relationship in a scatter diagram, when it was not sinking into my beebee brain at all. The next worst experience happened during the first Statistics test, as I watched the *Einstein's* of the class whip by me just fifteen minutes into the hour with their finished tests while I was still floundering around with the first problem. Could you blame me for coming unglued? Consider this question:

What is the binomial probability measure of gray offspring out of 200 produced from the mating of two flies? That might sound easy to some of you but not to me. How was I supposed to figure that out when I did not know what *binomial* meant?

By the end of the semester I looked like I had gone through the wringer of my mother's Maytag. More than once I questioned my sanity. I had not socialized in weeks. I forgot what my grandchildren looked like, and I suspected that my husband was ready to file suit. But, I continued torturing myself. I pestered the professor for help every day.

Truly, he was the most patient and understanding man - a regular modern day Job - who should be canonized before his demise for having me as a student. As you may have guessed, I just barely passed the course. In gratitude to the professor's undying devotion to my cause, I hereby dedicate the following satirical sonnet to him.

****

ODE TO STATISTICS

Statistics! Statistics! Thou maketh my day.
How I long for thy puzzling mathematica.
I see Thou in church on the white altar cloth.
I've grown into a bloomin' neurotica.
Mine husband sayeth he, art Thou thinking of me,
Whence thine eyes have that faraway stare?
Or art Thou lost in the path of that infamous math?
Doth thou still love me? Doth thou still care?
O' darling sweet mate, 'Tis that Quinsigamond State
Hath compelled me to learn mathematica.
Whence mine eyes look askew I'm not thinking of you,
I'm beguiled with that blessed Statistica.
O' my Statistica! O' my Statistics!
O' my Stats!

American Poetry Anthology, 1985

METRICS

ANOTHER SUBJECT THAT HAD ME bug-eyed was Metrics. First of all, how could anyone expect me to understand Metrics in one semester when it took me eight years to learn the multiplication tables? Second of all, why did I have to learn some European jargon when I barely understood American jargon? When I asked the professor for help, he directed me to room 378A for tutoring help. An audio-visual technician gave me a metrics kit with film strips explaining the entire metrics system. I expected that the strips would be boring but it turned out they were not boring at all, in fact, they were amusing as well as instructional. The title of the animated strips, *Gone Mit da Inch* by Ceecil Bee Deemile kept my interest to the very end. The first strip was narrated by a Ludwig von Drake character, who tells the tale of how our system of measurement began. "According to Drake, our present-day foot measurement started as a result of some land owner's bickering over property lines. Conflict arose because of the difference in the foot size of the people involved." Legend has it that in 1880, King Charlemagne's foot was used as a standard form of measurement to settle the dispute. Later, the difference between the nose and outstretched finger of King Edgar of England became the yard.

Sticks representing the foot and the yard were sent to villages everywhere and standardization began. The rest of the strip showed how other measurements came into use.

In the second strip, *The Mummy's Gloom,* a Groucho Marx voice tells the story of two explorers who try to uncover the secret of the Mummy's tomb. He then explains prefixes, abbreviations, and base units of the system. The last scene shows Leroy, Mrs. Teuton Geometric's little boy, looking for linen so he can change the sheets in his sarcophagus.

In strip number three, *Frankenstein Meets Litreman,* a Peter Lorre voice is heard teaching his sidekick, Hugo, how to use the litre for measuring volume and capacity. In typical horror movie fashion a monster is created.

The fourth strip, *The Maltese Chicken,* again narrated by Groucho shows a Humphrey Bogart character and a slick chick who foil a bank robbery. Groucho explains the meaning of a kilogram, the gram, and the difference between mass and weight. The Maltese chicken disappears and is later found after Groucho says the magic word.

The fifth strip, *a Day at the Chases,* or *Up at Metric Downs,* starring Groucho, is about a riverboat gambler and his experiences at the race track. Linear and cubic measures are explained as are centimeters and grams.

The sixth strip, *The Wizard of Metrics,* simulates a Judy Garland character who suddenly finds herself zapped in the Land of Metrics where she learns about measures for temperature, electricity, abbreviations, and symbols.

I enjoyed every minute of *Gone Mit da Inch.* What a unique way to teach Metrics - with humor. The reason I took Metrics is that in the eighties it was rumored that the American system of measurements would be changed to Metrics, and I did not want to be left in the lurch.

With all my math courses behind me I was sure the rest of the courses would be a cinch. Not so.

****

INTRO TO PSYCHOLOGY

I NEVER THOUGHT A *PSYCHE* course would throw me for a loop. I had difficulty with the course from day one. After a few botched-up tests I figured out a way to make things stick in my brain. On one test I had to explain internal and learned motivations related to hunger. I wrote the answers in free verse and adapted the words to the song, *Have You Seen My New Shoes,* sung by Shirley Temple in the movie *Captain January.* I recorded the song on a cassette tape. I listened to the tape while doing menial tasks, in the car, and every other chance I got in order for the words to sink in.The next part of the test had to do with Approach-Aproach Conflict, Avoidance-Conflict, and Approach-Avoidance Conflict. Again I wrote the answers in free-verse, and adapted the words to 76 *Trombones,* from the movie *Music Man.* I listened to the tape at every opportunity. I did the same thing for the rest of the test choosing songs that would fit with the words. On the day of the test I listened to the tape on the way to class. By now, the words were imbedded in my brain. I could hardly wait to get my hands on the little blue book. I wrote non-stop. I was elated when I saw a big red 94 on the cover of the blue book.

The method I devised was time-consuming, but it was well worth the effort. Another method, not quite as time-consuming is *chanting* the lessons. I wish I had come upon that method first. It worked like a charm. I used it for the rest of my studies with great results. Chanting my lessons led to high marks for the rest of my college days.

★★★★★★★

PERSONAL GROWTH

On the first day of class I thought, what could be difficult about personal growth? I was a full-grown mature woman. Not to worry. Oh yeah? That course took more out of me than my forty-five months of pregnancies. The nature of the course involved divulging my innermost thoughts and feelings. I was literally drained after each class. I did not want to look like a wimp in front of the younger students, so I volunteered information as they did. It was especially embarrassing when I self-disclosed something I never told anyone, or when I was in the spotlight for some time. At one point I was so shook up after role-playing that I was on the verge of tears. On one occasion I told the professor and the class that I lied when I was asked a question by one of the students. My face got beet red more than once during that course, but I was determined to jump right in, embarrassed or not.

During one of our classes the professor asked if we minded if anyone smoked. I said it did not bother me. (I lied) Why couldn't I tell the truth? Why couldn't I say that I minded at that point?

Further along in the course the question arose again, and this time I felt it was time to put my assertive skills into practice. I was proud of myself when I said I did mind if someone smoked, and I did it without offending the other person. I was growing.

Another incident happened outside of class when someone asked me to read a full-page off-color joke. I really did not want to read it but at risk of looking like a goody-two-shoes I read it, pretending I thought it was funny, and I actually forced a few laughs to make it look genuine. Hollywood here I come. I was mad at myself for not being assertive enough to say I was not interested. What in the world was wrong with me? I was relieved though when I heard testimonies by the students and the professor himself that they had experiences similar to mine.

Prior to taking *Personal Growth*, communicating, self-awareness, and assertiveness never entered my 57-year-old mind. Now, it is part of me and I have to stress that the one thing of utmost importance I have learned is that I have become aware of my innermost feelings. I had never tapped these feelings before. I just did not know how, or that they were important at all.

When I reflect on all this, who could possibly think about assertiveness while raising a family? Your whole body and soul is focused on your kids and your husband 24 hours a day, 365 days a year. That is what is nice about going to college in mid-life. The kids are out on their own, and the only other person around is your husband whose only concern is that you are home for supper.

****

PART III

ETCETERA

POTPOURI

This part of my book is a potpourri of manuscripts collected over the years that had been gathering dust in my files, while I was busy enjoying life with my husband Jerry and our five children, eight grandchildren, and one great-grandchild. Some of the stories are true, some are pure figments of my imagination, and some are a mixed bag of both.

Now and then, I took a breather to polish some of the manuscripts but they would go right back in my files to sort of simmer for another while. At one time I really got on the bandwagon and sent out articles, anecdotes, short stories, poems, and fiction. I would then create some new stuff and filed it for further revisions down the road, when I found time.

Well, time flew by and before I knew it my manuscripts were begging to be put into book form. Earlier on, I had planned to write a book of poems, a book of anecdotes, a book of essays, and a book of fiction. So here I am at age 79 and none of that is done! That's why I am piggy-backing on *Quinsigamond Tales, EtCetera,* hoping the transition from college experiences to life experiences will be a pleasant read.

****

REACHING FOR THE GOAL

When I made the commitment to get a college degree I knew there would be rough times ahead, but that did not deter me. I was eager to switch from low to high gear in the realm of the mind, and I was willing to jump in and test the waters whatever the outcome. I have to admit that some courses were difficult but I struggled along just the same. I felt comfortable in the world of academia. I just knew I belonged there. It was my place at that point in time. Some of my friends told me the reason they did not want to go to college was that they were afraid to fail. I told them they would never know if they did not try. I assured them that it really did not matter if they were not smart in school. It is what they have learned through their life experience that counts, and a strong desire to learn.

It is easy for me to say this now that it is all behind me, but honestly, there were days when absolutely nothing sank in at all, but I had my mind set and I persisted. At one point I identified with the TV commercial about drugs where two eggs are frying in a pan. A voice says, "This is your brain on drugs." Well that was my brain on books - fried! I reached for the goal anyhow. In the long run it was worth all the late night studying and everything else it took to achieve my goal. Yet, never once was I tempted to hang up my school bag because some of the courses were difficult. Yes, I had a school bag. My books had to be placed *just so* to expedite going to and from classes. I had to whip in and out of classes so quickly to get across campus that I was huffing and puffing all the time. Some days were terribly hectic, especially during the first semester. It was a dizzying schedule. Every morning before classes I posted a list on my bag with a schedule of classes to remind myself what day it was, what my next classroom number was, and what I had to pick up for supper on the way home.

I managed to keep my sanity to Commencement Day. Believe me. There was no greater experience than marching to *Pomp and Circumstance* with my fellow graduates, young and old, and no greater reward than to accept the navy blue folder with gold lettering that showed I had earned an Associate's degree in Liberal Arts with high honors. W-H-E-E-E! I DID IT!

After earning an Associate in Arts degree in 1982, I was eager to get back to studying and I enrolled at Worcester State College for one semester. I wrote the following poem as an assignment in a literature class.

****

JUST A BLACKBOARD

She knew six summers, and from her stance,
The big dark purplish panel scared her half to death.

Sometimes it looked blue-gray, depending on the weather,
Smooth sheet full of foreboding, so bully black.

Summoned every day to scratch the dank dark slate,
Her expertise in math, but she had none.

O' that she were David conquering the giant
With her little piece of chalk, but she could not.

Now she looks back.
Six decades of experience has changed all that.

Her childhood fears, erased by passing time,
Are as meaningless as the chalk dust

That
fell
upon
the
floor.

CCD KIDS, AN ENJOYABLE FEAST

WHEN I WAS SEVENTEEN THE Pastor of our church *volunteered* my services to teach a public school First Communion class. Me? The shy, shrinking little violet of the family get up in front of a class and T-E-A-C-H? I did not want to do it and I said, "B-but Father, I don't know how. P-please, take my sister, she's smart."

The Pastor completely ignored my pleas and handed me a Baltimore Catechism and said I was to start teaching the following Saturday. I wanted to die. My devious little mind hoped that the church and the school would burn down, or that my parents would suddenly decide to move back to Maine. It did not happen. I prayed all week that I would get sick and I would have to be replaced. That did not happen either.

Surprisingly, after I greeted the kids with a smile and a good morning, I felt a little more relaxed than when I went in. I taught them how to do the Sign of the Cross, recite the Our Father and the Hail Mary, and they read each in turn from the Catechism. They were all so well-behaved. I remember how they looked at me as they left the class smiling and waving. I felt so good after that first class that I looked forward to doing it again. That was 1941.

Time marched on to 1975. Having gone through high school, graduation, marriage, five kids and loads of free time to do my thing, I decided to volunteer as a Confraternity of Christian Doctrine teacher at my church. Their only need was for a sixth-grade teacher to instruct a class of twenty students in *The Scriptures*. I questioned the wisdom of my decision to take on a class of sixth-graders. This could be much different than the class of little ones I taught in 1941, and the subject was quite different also. However, I was familiar with the Scriptures because I had read them for many years, but I wondered if I could handle sixth graders.

The very first class was a disaster. The kids laughed when I mispronounced some of their names. A couple of the boys in the back row talked aloud and did not pay attention. They passed notes and made paper airplanes. I told them I would call the Pastor if they did not settle down. Unbeknownst to me the Pastor could hear what was going on through his office intercom. His booming voice threatened that he would call their parents to come to the school to pick them up if they did not behave. After that the students simmered down a bit.

The following week I told the Pastor I did not think I could continue, but he asked me to try again and I did. I requested that the class be moved from the traditional rows of seats to the library where we could sit on the rug in a circle. I thought if the kids were in a more relaxed setting they would behave better. Well, the next class was not without trepidation. Some of the boys looked out the window amused by two cats carousing in the grass. The girls giggled at the boys. Two basketball enthusiasts flung the ball across the room until I retrieved it. A group of girls babbled about a recent party, while I attempted to begin class with a prayer and I ended up by yelling, "Q-U-I-E-T!"

The most frustrating experience of all was after I had spent the whole week giving my wall-to-wall application to *The Boy Joseph* lesson, multi-colored beach towel and all, and my plans went awry when the other sixth-grade teacher called in sick, and instead of twenty kids I suddenly had forty! Well, I'm no Billy Graham so after a few nervous moments I told the kids to open their books to the song section. We sang all the songs over and over. My first thought was to have the kids walk around the schoolyard play-acting the Exodus, but it was raining. Yet, all was not lost. At the end of class I packed my bags relieved in a sense that next week's lesson was ready. Praise God. As I turned the ignition key and started for home I reflected on the previous hour's happenings. I thought about the adage: WHEN YOU HAVE A LEMON, MAKE LEMONADE. It pleased me to know that there were forty kids out there who were not likely to forget the lesson they learned in song. Excerpts follow.

Who made the world we live in, who gave us all the things we're given. God spoke to us from the dawn of history when he gave certain men the gift of prophecy. Abraham dwelt in the land of Chaldea. Joseph's brothers tried to put an end to his dreams. The Lord is my shepherd, nothing shall I want. When Israel was in Egypt's land oppressed so hard they could not stand, let my people go.

The following week I anticipated the students' acting out *The Boy Joseph*. Unfortunately, the lead character was not fit for the part. As soon as I gave him the multi-colored beach towel he wrapped it around himself and ran around the library in an attempt to run away from his *brothers*. That's when I summoned the Pastor who put an end to the ruckus by taking *Joseph* to his office for strict disciplining. Thereafter, I decided to stick with the curriculum. No more dramatic stuff.

When our Coordinator showed some slides on *The Life of Christ,* the kids took notes for a future essay. The following excerpts were excellent, showing that they were fully absorbed, but the spelling, Oh! When Jon the basset batized jeses in the jordin he was felled with the holee speerit. Geesis tawt in sinagogs and preecht the good noose. Jezus wawked along the see of galary. They bleevd that Jeezus was the promist masiya. He heeled siknes and dazeeze. Today Jakups well haswotter for traflers.

Although the spelling was wrong, I considered these bits of sentences little gems. It showed that the message was clear in their minds, and that the slides impressed them.

The enjoyable part of CCD classes came with the humorous *asides.* One Saturday morning while discussing the Sacrament of Penance, tying it in with the story of Joseph and reconciliation, one of the kids asked, "Do you have false teeth?" Then right on the heels of that question came, "What's that blue stuff all over your eyelashes?" To the first question I answered "Yes." And to the second question I said, "Maybelline, and back to the Sacrament of Penance."

Yes, teaching CCD is enjoyable, and the fascination it has for me is hard to describe. True, it's not all peachy-keen and rosy as my peers will admit, but it has its rewards. For me, it lies in the hope that I have touched their hearts with the love I have for God, for my country and for my fellow man. I hope that someday these students will become CCD teachers too. Only then will they know about the *enjoyable feast* I have experienced.

****

Marian Helpers Bulletin, October-December 1979

THE SADDEST DAY
NOVEMBER 22, 1963

IT WAS A BRISK, SUNNY November day. The kids had returned to school after lunch and I looked forward to an afternoon of peace and quiet. I turned the radio on unaware that what I was about to hear would change the course of events for the nation and the world. I was overwhelmed and saddened by the grim news. Reluctantly, I turned the TV on. CBS news anchor Walter Cronkite announced that John F. Kennedy, the President of the United States had been assassinated.

Soon a weary nation was engulfed in tears. During the next few days everything I did seemed surreal. I ate, but I hardly tasted the food. I talked, but I did not fully communicate. I did housework, but I hardly paid heed to the task. People went to church in droves to pray for comfort but it was not there. There was no consolation for our grief. Through the days that followed until Taps was sounded at Arlington, we relived the events over and over again. Raindrops of sadness had drowned us in sorrow.

People from all over the world came and wept. And through the modern marvel of television we were on the scene of action every minute of the day. The funeral procession impressed me deeply. I cried at the steady beat of the drums and the marching feet of Jacqueline Kennedy, John, Caroline, family and world dignitaries.

All marching forward in the dismal parade fashioned after the funeral of President Abraham Lincoln one-hundred years ago.

Although Jacqueline Kennedy did not cry openly, her heart must have shed many tears. Her sad expression reflected the torment of her soul. The following Monday, devotions were held in many places of worship. Catholics, Protestants, Jews, and other denominations, all from different faiths yet all united to pay tribute to President Kennedy.

Indeed we have lost a great man. He will live in the memories of all living people as well as in the history pages of generations not yet embryonic. Ironically, neither Lincoln nor Kennedy, in their lifetime, accomplished what they set out to achieve - equality of men. The words, "Let us begin," were part of Kennedy's Inaugural Address. There is a message there. Let us begin to love one another, and treat every race, color, and creed as God intended. Let us not hand down to future generations the stuff that wars are made of - greed, hatred, and lust for power.

Though the tears are dry, and the bustle of daily living is in full swing, our hearts will always cry a little, when our thoughts bring us back to *The Saddest Day.*

★★★★★★★

ONCE UPON A TIME

Once upon a time I had an English nun-teacher who yelled constantly, "Never start a composition with Once upon a time!" Sister Imelda made a lasting impression on me, because while she yelled she waved her whip-stick frantically in the air. She called her whipstick Josephine and it did not phase her to use it if anyone got out of hand. It was a long, smooth wooden pointer to which she had sadistically attached some shredded leather strips for effects. Everyone was afraid to move for fear they would get the Josephine. And no one dared to start a composition with Once upon a time, either.

The only reason I am braving it today is that I heard Sister Imelda has gone to her *just reward.* I thought she was ninety-nine then! I keep wondering which way she went, since flagellation constitutes a mortal sin of the worst kind. I think she should do at least ten years in Purgatory and then get transferred to Hades, never mind being rewarded by going to heaven.

Sister hovered over us during Palmer Method practice. What a grouch. If we went over the lines she would grab the paper, wrinkle it into a ball, throw it on the floor and growl, "Start over!" She made me very nervous.

One day I darn near swallowed a marble because of her. I was rolling a marble around in my mouth (don't ask me why) when Sister asked, "What are you eating?"

"N-nothing." I garbled.

When I started to choke Sister gave me a whack on the back and the marble flew out of my mouth. Then she embarrassed to death by making me kneel down in the corner for disturbing the class. How I ever made it out of grammar school with a full box of matches is beyond me.

After an especially busy Josephine-waving-day, my friend Adella and I grumbled as we walked out of class about what a royal pain in the neck Sister Imelda was.

"What a witch." I said. "She could go to a Halloween party without a mask."

"Yah." Echoed Adella. "She'd win first prize for *most ugly*."

Unbeknownst to us Sister was behind us and heard every word. She chased us all the way down Illinois Street waving her Josephine, but we outran her by a few laps. We laughed about it all the way home. I never forgot Sister Imelda and her whipstick named Josephine and I never started a composition with Once upon a time either - until today.

****

THE WAY WE WERE

SISTER IMELDA'S BLACK MUSLIN VEIL always smelled of No. 2 pencils and chalk dust. The strange mixture of odors intensified when she flipped her veil backward to get it out of her face as she walked past me. It was worse when she bent over my desk in sixth grade French class and scolded me for putting the accent marks in the wrong place. When that black spectre of cloth touched my shoulders, I shivered. It felt like I was actually wearing the veil. She always wanted one of us Boucher girls to enter the convent. Well, that was the last place *this* Boucher girl wanted to go. I figured she could work on my sister Michelle, because I had no intention of joining a religious order, one reason being that I didn't think I was smart enough to teach and the other reason being that I was afraid I would end up in the kitchen as a cook. For the life of me I could not understand how anyone could be holed-up in a convent. The only places nuns ever went (as far as I knew) was to school, to church, and to retreats. To me their whole existence was a retreat.

The mind-set of the times was such that as little kids we believed that nuns and priests were saints who were put here by God to guide us so we would not go astray. And believe it or not, I thought nuns did not have any private parts and that they never went to the bathroom . I just could not picture nuns going to such a place as *the toilet*. And the mere idea that nuns and priests were go-betweens with God scared the living daylights out of me.

My sister Michelle and I were madly in love with the Thibeau twins. Every chance we got we met them in Crystal Park, across the street from school and church. Once, during Lent, we met them by the pond instead of going to Mass. We got caught. My brother Eddie was cutting through the park to go to work and saw us. He swore he would never squeal on us. We were scared. Skipping Mass during Lent was a serious offense, and our mothers would have punished us severely if they knew.

Sometimes after school Michelle and I would go to my girlfriend Adella's house to listen to *Mary Noble, Backstage Wife* on the radio. Our mother would not allow us to listen to those filthy soap operas. When we got home we said we had to stay after school to erase the blackboards. (Little liars). We were model students in class, but we were mischievous on the outside. Once, I got punished for bringing a deck of cards to school. Another time Michelle and I got sent to the Superior's office during recess for tap-dancing on the convent porch. And when we crossed the white line in the schoolyard to talk to the boys we were punished by having to write: I will not cross the white line ever again, twenty times on the blackboard.

I hated to see Fridays come. That was the day we two-by-two'd it to confession. We could not talk in ranks. We had to reflect on our sins and practice the formula for confession so as not to annoy the priest with hesitations. Michelle and I, like many other kids, made up sin lists and swapped them. When I parted the heavy velvet maroon drapes and entered the dark cedar-wood enclosure, I felt like throwing up. It seemed like an eternity before the priest gave the other confessee absolution. ZAP! A miniature sliding door slammed open. My inquisition. Oh, God! The priest's ear was glued to the screen and my nose was so close I could smell his ear wax.

The reason I got so close to the screen is that Sister stood next to the drape to guide the next kid in. I did not want her to hear my sins. I made the sign of the cross and stammered, "B-Bless me F-Father for I have sinned. It has been one week since my l-last confession. These are m-my sins."

"How many times?"

"Three t-times."

"Speak louder child."

"Three t-times."

Gee whiz, I thought, these aren't even my sins. The priest gave me penance and absolution and commanded, "Go! And sin no more!"

For my penance I had to say three Our Father's, three Hail Mary's, and three Glory Be's. I had to say the Act of Contrition, kiss the foot of the cross, and genuflect before the main altar before I went back to my seat. Then I had to pray the Stations of the Cross. An so it went every Friday until I got out of grammar school.

My high school years went by like a flash. Now I could decide what I wanted to do with the rest of my life, but my mother and Sister Imelda had already decided that I should enter the convent. "I'd rather go to jail!" I protested. "I'm not going to no nun Academy."

My mother and Sister Imelda made me feel so guilty - AFTER ALL THEY DID FOR ME - that I gave in. It did not help that my Aunt Elizabeth had two girls in a cloistered order in New Hamshire, my Aunt Maryjane had two girls in a teaching order in Maine, and my Aunt Angelina had a daughter/nun in Canada.

"It's in your genes my child." Sister Imelda said as she squeezed me by the shoulders to reassure me. To deny my mother the honor of becoming a nun would have been unforgivable in everyone's eyes. I enrolled at the Academy and everyone was happy except me. My schedule revolved around praying and studying, and more praying and studying. I hated it. We did everything in the same order every day. Up at five, meditations, Mass, breakfast, chores, classes, chapel, lunch, classes, chapel, supper, study, chapel, and lights out at nine o'clock.

I was so homesick. I missed my mother's cooking, my father's joking, and I even missed fighting with Michelle over who's turn it was to do the dishes or make the beds. After what seemed like a hundred years I became a postulant. I was very unhappy but I tried not to show it. I just went through the motions, all the while I kept asking myself why I continued to live this farce. I could not go on living a lie much longer. I was deceiving myself, my mother, and Sister Imelda. I decided to put an end to the years of unhappiness I had gone through. The rigidness of convent life was too much to bear.

One night I packed my belongings in my little black suitcase and waited for nine o'clock. In stocking feet I tip-toed down the long shiny hardwood floor to the steps that led downstairs. I turned the knob slowly and went out into the cool October air to freedom. Nervously, I put on my shoes, left my shoelaces untied and hurried down the dark narrow street that led to the bus stop. I took off my veil, removed the stiff white band that encircled my face, and wrapped the veil around my head like a kerchief. I had just enough money for bus fare to Millville where my friend Adella lived. It was ten o'clock when I rang her doorbell. "Oh, my God, what are you doing here?"

"Oh, Adella, I left the convent. I couldn't stand it there anymore."

Adella hugged me and held me tight. I began to cry uncontrollably.

"How did you get out? Tell me all about it."

We sat at the kitchen table, sipped tea and talked for hours about everything. I planned to call home and the convent, but by then an all-points bulletin had gone out on all local radio stations about a missing nun. I called home, the convent and the police. My mother and Sister Imelda were devastated by what I had done. I did not think they would ever forgive me. It took them a long time, but they finally realized convent life was not for me. Then my mother and Sister Imelda started to work on Michelle. I knew they thought she was more pious than I was. Should I tell them about the lies, the sin lists, the Thibeau twins in Crystal Park?

****

THE PSYCHOLOGY OF AGING

As much as I loved writing and sending manuscripts to publishers I was beginning to miss academia, and in 1984 I enrolled at Assumption College in Worcester, in their Continuing Education Program. I loved it. While there I took the following courses: Bible, Hollywood Western, Creative Writing, Professional and Academic Writing, Oil Painting, Acrylic Painting, Spanish I & II, Ethical Thinking, The Study of the Art Museum Collection, Visual Experience, Children's Literature, Major American Authors, and the Psychology of Aging.

Going to college nights is different from being a full-time day student. It just drags on at a turtle's pace and you think you will never see graduation day. It took seven years to earn my B.A. in Liberal Studies. Since I was already past mid-life I was anxious to take *The Psychology of Aging* to learn what to expect in my old age. What an eye-opener. The course shed much light on issues I had privately moaned and groaned about as I approached maturity. It pleased me to hear from a young instructor about the myths of aging. A licensed social worker and instructor at Assumption College, he worked in a local nursing home during the day, so he had first-hand knowledge about the subject of aging.

He pointed out how unfortunate it is that we live in a number-oriented society, and he deplored the negative attitudes regarding chronological age. He wanted to change that. But sadly, he died suddenly the week before the finals cutting short the plans he had to make a better life for the elderly.

In one of his lectures the instructor noted that when some young people see an older man who is losing his hair they say he is getting bald. Yet, when those same young people see a young man who is losing his hair, they say he has a receding hair line. When an older man repeats himself it does not always mean he is getting senile, chances are he knows he said it before, but it just happens to fit the conversation. Yet, some young people are quick to judge that he is *losing it.*

Another area where older persons are not given a fair shake according the instructor, is in the questions they are asked during Alzheimers evaluations. When the interviewer asks patients what they had for supper the night before, some of them do not remember. Sometimes it is only because they are put on the spot. If those patients asked the interviewer what they had, they probably would not remember either. In one of his classes the instructor put the younger students to the test. The same Alzheimers questions were given to 20 and 30-year olds. Guess what? Some of them fared no better than the older patients. Some of them did not remember what they had for supper the night before, or remember who the President was last election.

According to the instructor, many older persons are misdiagnosed with Alzheimers disease. He emphasized that a great deal of revamping needs to be done cocerning those tests. He further noted our age-oriented society labels people according to their chronological age. As mentioned before, many older persons repeat stories over and over. He said that older persons go through what he called *life review.* They enjoy telling stories over again. They have lived a long time and they have so much to offer the next generation.

What an opportunity for young people to tape their conversations for posterity. Another sad aspect about growing older is that there are far too many persons kept alive on drugs, suffer, then die in a vegetative state. "We need to fix that." The instructor said.

Back to chronological age. A 60-year-old who acts like 40 is no doubt young in mind, heart, and spirit, with a positive outlook on life. People with such a mentality stay *forever young* , wrinkles and all. Just because someone is over 60 does not mean it is time to slow down, to me it is time to *Rev Up!* I look up to Grandma Moses. She is my role model. She was well into her 80's when she started to paint. James Michener kept on writing in his 80's. I read that he could not wait to get up in the morning because he had so many exciting things to do. A 93-year-old woman in Florida went hang-gliding. Before she took the leap her daughter said, "You can't do that! You're too old, and your bones are brittle."

To which the mother answered, "They are not!"

I could fill pages about people over 60 who have not let their chronological age interfere with doing what they want to do. If they are healthy, anything is possible!

Permit me to air my views about the Senior Citizen label. I wonder who coined that phrase. Well, if it is all right with you I am going to coin a few more to add to it. Since people over 60 are labeled Senior Citizens, why not label the Baby Boomers Junior Citizens, the X Generation Sophomore citizens, and the rest of society Freshman Citizens? Sound crazy? I do not think so. For a society that is hung up on chronological age I think it is quite fitting. What is good for one segment of our society should be good for all, don't you agree?

Learning something new for me never ends. Since earning an A.A. and a B.A. I have returned for the following courses: Public Speaking, Fiction Writing, and Computer classes. It took me seven years to earn my B.A degree. I never for a moment regretted any of it. I would do it again - in a heartbeat.

★★★★★★★

MADE IN THE SHADE

When the editor of a top slick magazine sent me a note which read: We are holding your article for consideration, I just knew I had arrived as a freelancer and that I had it *made in the shade.* I had been studying that particular slick reading every word from cover to cover. My reason for wanting to break into that magazine was that I liked the writing style of the women authors, because they wrote just like me. HA!

I visualized a bright future. Me, a nobody, finally making it big. What a success story. I made mental pictures of myself autographing the Great American Novel I started in 1968. When I get rich, I dreamed, I will buy a mansion on the Cape and spend all my time writing from my veranda overlooking the Atlantic. My husband and five kids would have to make appointments to see me. Well, I can't be everywhere if I am flitting to Chicago and California to appear on talk shows.

It is 2:30 pm. I hear two bells ringing. The kids are at the back door and the mailman is at the front door. I let the kids in and dash for the mail. My eyes immediately catch sight of a number ten envelope with the publisher's return address.

Since I make copies of manuscripts to save on return postage, I inform the publishers to destroy the manuscript if they reject it. So, I never know by the envelope if it is a check or a rejection. Please let it be a check, please, please. It was from the editor saying my article did not fit their current needs.

Suddenly, I hate words. I think about giving up this whole writing business. I am envious of Erma Bombeck. I am sure her father is a publisher with pull and that is how she got in. That's it. I quit! All the while my little boy Stevie is waving a paper for me to read. I grab it out of his hand impatiently and yell, "WHAT IS IT?"

"It's something the teacher dictated to us and I have to learn it by heart."

It read: I plejaleejince to the flag of thee yoonited stakes of Umerica. I suppressed a smile and thought, hey, I could use this in an article on illiteracy in our schools. See that, I just cannot leave an idea alone. I will probably get another rejection, but I don't care.

Writing is fun, and a great learning experience. The fun part is creating something totally new, and the learning is in revising, polishing, and making my stuff ready for the printed page. And if Fanny Hurst can receive thirty-five rejections from the *Saturday Evening Post* and finally get the green light on the thirty-sixth, so can I. And with dogged determination and the will to succeed, I know that someday soon I will have it *made in the shade.*

****

I REACHED FOR THE STARS AND LANDED IN THE BUSHES

AFTER READING ABOUT A WRITER who reached for the stars and landed on top of the trees, I reached for the stars too, but I landed in the bushes. On a whim I sent an 80-word anecdote to *The Family Digest* magazine. It sold on sight for $5.00. I jumped up and down in the kitchen with the check in my hand. When I came down from my high I ran to my files and got right down to business. I sent another anecdote to the same magazine. Zap. Another sale, another $5.00. I was stunned by my instant success and confident that my road to the top would be smooth. Little did I realize that my first two sales the first time out was pure beginner's luck. I became a slave to writing, barely taking time to eat. I sent one manuscript out after another. At one time I had 25 manuscripts on the road from Maine to California. Cooking meals became an intrusion and I resented it. As a result there was nothing creative about what I put on the table. I am surprised my husband did not leave me. Hey, I was a gifted writer, what did he expect?

To my dismay all 25 manuscripts were rejected. My ego was crushed beyond recognition. I made faces at the editor's names on the rejection slips. My Gethsemany. Why hast Thou forsaken me, O Lord? Then the brazen side of me took hold. The Syndicates!

Why didn't I think of that before? Convinced that I was just as funny as Erma Bombeck, I sent 6 columns to the syndicate that published *At Wit's End*. (Bombeck's publisher). Can you believe my stupidity? What would that publisher want with the likes of me, an unknown, when he already had the top funny lady in the field? I scrapped that idea when I received the 6 columns back pronto. That should have told me something. What did I know about the publishing business? Not much. Down deep I knew something was wrong with my *creations.* I knew how to put my ideas on paper, but that was hardly enough. I called a magazine circulation office and poured out my tale of woe to a total stranger who advised me to subscribe to the *Writer's Digest* magazine. I have been grateful to her ever since. Thanks a million, wherever you are. I read every inch of every issue for 6 months, highlighting information, suggestions, ideas, markets, and contests. I signed up for an article writing course and learned things I never knew about the art of writing. I studied the pulps, the slicks and the newspapers. I analyzed my rejected manuscripts. The flaws were many. I profitted by the following *do nots.* Do not send a manuscript out when it is hot off your creative wire. It is not ready. Revise and polish it umpteen times. Do not ignore publishers guidelines. Pay attention to every word. Do not mail a manuscript without a SASE. You will never see it again. Do not ramble on with three sentences when you could do it with one. Write tight. Do not send a manuscript written in longhand. No one will read it. Do not call the editor unless you are a well-known author. He/she doesn't have time for such things. Do not send sloppy copies with typos. A rejection will follow. Do not let your relatives read your manuscripts. They will praise them to the hilt. Lastly, do not let a few sales go to your head. Hang in there and work. It will be worth it.

I revised and polished my manuscripts until I was blue in the face. At one point I could wallpaper all the rooms in my house with pages of stuff I did not like and discarded. Hard work? You bet. But, believe me, it was worth every minute of it.

After awhile things began to change. I began to sell. Thrilled by my success, I sometimes hit the sack at three in the morning. Soon the bags under my eyes had baggies. I reasoned that if things got worse I could always wear a mask. I was willing to go that far. My husband thought I was out of my mind. He was sure I would be dead and buried soon if I kept up such a pace. It was all worth the struggle. I read somewhere that there is no elevator ride to success - you have to take the stairs. Happy climbing!

★★★★★★★

"Writing is easy. All you have to do is cross off the wrong words."

-Mark Twain

A HOUSEWIFE/WRITER - THE UPSIDE

The American Heritage Dictionary circa 1984, defines a housewife as a married woman who supervises the affairs of a household. Its definition of the word *writer* is one who writes esp. as an occupation or profession; author. These are jobs like any other job. But, when you tell someone you are writing a book they look at you with a blank stare like they are thinking - what a nice little hobby. As my writer friends will attest, it is a very real job. And this essay is for the purpose of flaunting the pluses of being a housewife/writer.

For one thing I am glad I do not have to look spiffy for a 9-5 job. I do not have to get up before the birds in winter to brush snow piles off the car. I do not have to fight traffic to and from work. And best of all I do not have to put up with a head honcho boss who thinks he is God's gift to womankind.

Yup. As a housewife/writer I am my own boss. I can lounge around in my pajamas, drink x cups of coffee and write all day if I choose to. Housework is not my favorite *indoor sport* so I clean just ten minutes in each room. I set the kitchen timer and stop when the bell rings. Ten minutes is all those inanimate objects deserve from me.

Then I sit at my iMac and write to my heart's content. Around three o'clock I close the door of my *Word Shop* to start supper.

The only out I have is food shopping day, Scrabble day, and volunteer day. Socializing is not usually my thing, but last year my husband and I went to my 50th grammar school reunion. Surprisingly, the boy-crazy girl who stole all our boyfriends ended up an old maid, the boy *most likely* was a job-hopper who never settled down, and the smartest girl in class didn't even have a job. I was the only *writer* in the group. When I told them I was a published author of articles and short stories, and that someday I was going to write a book, they all looked at me with a blank stare and one of them said, "You're a w-h-a-t? I could tell they were not impressed because they continued to chit-chat and sipped away on their highballs. When we got home I was in a lousy mood, but my spirits were lifted when I caught sight of a saying on my bulletin board.

"TO START TO WRITE IS TO START TO LIVE, BECAUSE IT IS TO START TO OBSERVE AND PITY AND LOVE AND ADORE AND SING."

-Robert Fontaine

****

GRANDMOTHER AND THE BEADS

My maternal grandmother was quite a lady. And she was très influential especially in religious matters. At our house we said the beads every night with grandmother, my parents, and my nine brothers and sisters. However, the practice of saying the beads always seemed to happen just when something important was at hand, and no matter what our plans were we could not leave until we said the beads. If our friends came over during that time they had to kneel and pray with us. Absolutely nothing interfered with the beads, but sometimes the beads put a stop to our squabbles cutting them short as soon as grandmother called us into the parlor. We certainly could not fight while praying, but sometimes an aborted argument resumed as soon as we got up off our knees.

Grandmother, born of Protestant parents and orphaned at age five, was adopted by a Catholic family and became a convert to the Catholic faith. She often referred to her biological parents as *Black Protestants.* And for the longest time I thought my ancestors were from Africa. As I got older, however, I realized the expression meant that believers were so strong in their faith they could not be swayed otherwise.

After my grandfather died, grandmother broke up housekeeping and sort of *took to the road*. Really. She would pack her suitcase after a six-month hitch, and she would be off to another relative's house for another vacation. She was like a traveling Marian missionary, bringing her faith and her beads to another houseful of relatives.

Saying the beads sometimes got in the way of my patriotic endeavors during World War II. Nurse's were scarce because of the overseas demand for them, so my girlfriend Adella and I joined a volunteer Red Cross Nurse's Aide Program. Among other things we were trained to go out during air-raid practice. I secretly wished for an emergency so I could really get into the act. I got my wish one night when the shop-horns at Brown Shoe signaled an air-raid practice. Grandmother had already started the beads and everyone was in the parlor except me. I was in the kitchen when I heard the *Je croix en Dieu* loud and clear, but I tried to sneak out by the back door. Grandmother stopped the beads abruptly and ordered me into the parlor and on my knees. I swear she could see right through the walls.

Grudgingly, I answered the Hail Mary's, the Our Father's and the Glory Be's. It seemed like an hour before the last Glory Be. It seemed like another hour by the time grandmother got through the Beatitudes and the Pray for us's. When we were finished with the beads the air-raid practice was over. I left for the hospital feeling resentful toward grandmother. Going out in pitch dark would have been really exciting. That night when I got home from the hospital I saw grandmother's suitcase packed and ready to go. She was leaving the next day for a hitch with my Aunt Maryjane in Maine. My devious little mind entertained thoughts of freedom for the next 6 months.

Instilled with the patriotic fervor of the times, I quit my job as an office clerk at Norton Company and went to work at St. Pierre Chain, a defense plant, where I became a lady-welder linking large anchor chains for the Navy.

I looked like Rosie the Riveter with my blue overalls, protective metal hood; welding torch, and my over-sized gray canvas gloves.

Against our parents wishes my girlfriend Adella and I decided to join a branch of the service. I would join the WACS and Adella would join the WAVES. We went to the recruiting office and much to our dismay found out that we were too young (18) to join any branch of the service. Applicants had to be U.S. citizens between the ages of 21 and 45 with no dependents, be at least five feet tall, and weigh 100 pounds or more. We fulfilled all of the above except our age. So we went our merry way and kept service men's morale's up by going to USO Club dances and dated soldiers, sailors, coast guardsmen, and marines, when they were on leave.

When the war ended in 1945, my patriotic endeavors ended also, but saying the beads went on even when grandmother was not there. Grandmother lived to the ripe old age of ninety-six and fortunately, I have preserved black and white movies of her holding her beads and squinting from the floodlights of my 8mm Brownie movie camera. In retrospect, the disappointments I experienced during the seemingly demanding practice of saying the beads with grandmother, is now a pleasant memory.

If any one of our five children becomes a writer, he or she just might write a sequel to this story, because the practice of saying the beads handed down by my grandmother and my mother, will most likely be part of their fond memories. They will probably complain that I made them kneel down every night to say the beads. And worst of all, if their friends came over while we were praying, they had to kneel down too - in the sixties for crimminy sakes! Be assured they are none the worse for wear for the experience, and they do not have arthritis of the knees from their mother-inflicted ritual.

After *Vatican Two,* when the ritual of saying the beads was no longer in practicce in our churches it also phased out of our lives, but my mother's blue crystal beads, draped around the neck of my Pieta statue, reminds me of a time when life was simple. And sometimes in moments of solitude I finger my mother's beads and say them to myself and I am back there in time, and I am young again.

****

Queen of All Hearts, September-October, 1992

THE GOLD PENDANT

THE YEAR WAS 1942. HOLY Family High school graduation practice exercises were in full swing at the all-girl school I attended. We talked about the graduation dresses our mothers were sewing. We snickered about the style behind Sister's back because we thought it was terribly old-fashioned. But Sister Superior had the last say about the pattern chosen. It had to be modest, high-necked and long-sleeved. Then we talked about the graduation presents we thought we would be getting with great excitement. My friend Adella had already received her graduation present from her parents, a beautiful gold Bulova watch. I was happy for her, but I was upset when I found out that all the other girls were getting watches too. I did not think I would be getting one.

My parents had not talked about what they planned as a gift for me and I wondered if they had been skimping and saving to surprise me on graduation night with a watch. I knew they were struggling to make ends meet, but when I got home, I told them what all the other girls were getting. They told me they could not possibly afford such a luxury. In the 40's watches were expensive. *Timex* had not yet made the scene.

On graduation night I tried hard not to show my disappointment at the 14-carat gold pendant my parents bought on credit at Kay's Jewelry store for 50 cents a week. The pendant was about the size of a penny, very thin and smooth to the touch, and very pretty on its slim gold chain. I wore it on graduation night feeling embarrassed because my parents could not afford a watch for me. As the girls showed their watches to each other, I made an excuse to go to the Rest Room where I cried in self-pity for some time. I vowed then and there that I would buy myself a watch as soon as I got a job and saved up enough money. After graduation night I did not wear the pendant very often. I am sure my parents were deeply hurt by my attitude toward the pendant, but they did not show it outwardly.

The year is 1980. My parents are long since dead. Thirty-eight years have passed since graduation night. I have had many watches in that span of time - gold ones, silver ones, and bangle ones. Now I could care less if I even wear one. More and more over the years I have worn the gold pendant, and it has come to mean a whole lot more to me than all the throw-away watches I have had since they came in vogue.

My gold pendant, given to me out of great sacrifice to my parents, grows more dear to me as time goes by. It is by far my favorite piece of jewelry. I have never seen another that could match its beautiful simplicity. I wear it proudly. Thanks Mom and Dad.

Worcester Sunday Telegram Talent Page 1985

(The following story is a fictionalized version of *The Gold Pendant)*

THANKS, MOM AND DAD

EMERALD SQUARE MALL WAS A favorite Saturday hangout for Joanna and her two girlfriends, Chris and Kelly. Melodious music and a medley of shoppers voices greeted them as they entered. The smell of chocolate chip cookies enticed them to follow their noses to the goodies. Besides shopping and eating, they enjoyed gawking at the cool dudes in Olympic Sports.

"Three cookies and three Diet Pepsi's please?" Chris told the clerk as she motioned to Kelly and Joanna that she was buying.

"Gee thanks." They both said.

"Let's sit here." Chris said as she walked toward a long wooden bench.

Kelly sank her teeth into a cookie. "M-m-m, these are yummy."

"Decadent," Joanna commented, "it's like dying and going to cookie heaven."

They gulped down their drinks and threw the empties in a trash barrel.

"C'mon Joanna," Chris said, "we want to show you what we're getting for graduation gifts from our parents."

"Yah." Echoed Kelly.

"Well, what is it?" Joanna asked impatiently.

"You'll see," Kelly said, "over there at Zales, they are so cool."

The trio headed for the watch display case. Joanna's eyes popped when her friends pointed to the Gucci watches displayed on rich black velvet props.

"Wow! You gotta be kidding." Joanna raved.

The gold link bracelet sport watches glistened through the case, and the price tag of $200.00 gave Joanna a sinking feeling in her stomach. Joanna knew that getting a Gucci watch from her parents was out of the question. They were struggling just to get by. What upset Joanna most was that Chris and Kelly were trend-setters and whatever they got, the other graduates would most likely get too. As they left Zales, Joanna still had hopes that maybe her parents had been saving to surprise her with a Gucci watch. When Chris and Kelly tried on earrings and hair ornaments at Scribbles, Joanna showed no interest. She tagged along slowly, feeling lousy inside. The next stop was the Video Store. The girls were not planning to buy videos they just wanted to feast their eyes on the *hunk* behind the counter - a dead-ringer for Vanilla Ice. Joanna only pretended to be interested. After browsing in practically all the stores they went to Papa Gino's and ordered a large pepperoni pizza. When Joanna got home she told her parents what Chris and Kelly were getting as graduation gifts.

"Two-hundred-dollars!" Her mother gasped.

"Don't you understand," her father said, "you know I'm out of work, and who knows if I'll ever get called back to the plant." He shook his head in disgust.

Joanna went to her room, slammed the door and flopped face down on the bed and cried. She resented the fact that her father was not working. The recession had not affected Chris's and Kelly's parents who had secure jobs. They had all the luxuries anyone could want. After wiping her eyes Joanna leafed through some teen magazines and tried to forget what just happened.

On graduation night Joanna tried hard not to show her disappointment at the 14-carat gold locket her parents charged at Kay Jewelers for 50 cents a week. It was plain to see however, that Joanna was not elated. The locket, about the size of a penny, was thin, embossed with a leaf design, and very pretty on its slim gold chain. Joanna wasn't impressed. The other five girls in her class got Gucci watches. After graduation ceremories Joanna made an excuse to go to the restroom where she cried her eyes out. She decided then and there that she would buy herself a Gucci watch as soon as she got a job and saved up enough money.

A party at Chris's lasted until three in the morning. They munched on goodies, drank strawberry punch, smoked Virginia Slims, and signed yearbooks - a parting of the ways - the end of their fun times together. That night Joanna put the royal blue velvet jewelry box in her dresser drawer. She didn't want to think about it anymore. Joanna knew her parents were deeply hurt by her attitude toward the locket, but she never tried to make them feel better about the whole thing.

Chris and Kelly went away to college. Joanna went to work at Scribbles. She opened a savings account; deposited ten dollars each week, kept enough for bus fare and gave the rest to her parents. Joanna would have her Gucci watch at last - she thought. When her father's unemployment benefits ran out, Joanna grudgingly gave her entire paycheck at home, otherwise they would have to go on welfare assistance. Many months later Joanna's father got called back to work and she was allowed to keep her entire pay check. Soon, Joanna had enough money to buy the watch.

"Look Ma, look Dad, I got my Gucci watch isn't it a beauty?" Joanna boasted. Her parents tried to look impressed but the watch would always remind them that they could not buy it for her. That night Joanna wrote letters to Chris and Kelly telling them about the watch. She lit a cigarrette and propped herself up on the fluffy foam pillows she bought at Bed & Bath. She put the watch under her pillow, closed her eyes and imagined herself showing it off to her friends at work the next day. Joanna fell asleep. The bedding caught fire. She awoke coughing and gasping for breath and ran quickly out of the smoke-filled room. Lucky for Joanna the smoke alarm kicked in to warn her. By the time the firemen came the mattress was engulfed in flames. They threw the mattress out the window. Joanna knew her Gucci watch was destroyed, but her gold locket, still in its royal blue velvet case was in the drawer where she put it on graduation night.

She hardly wore the locket, because it would bring back unpleasant memories of her graduation. When she opened the case the locket was tilted on its white satin prop. As she cried on graduation night, she now cried at how much she must have hurt her parent's feelings for the only gift they could afford for her. Feelings of deep remorse crept over her. She remembered that she hardly wore the locket and never thanked her Mom and Dad for the graduation gift they were still making payments on. She fastened the locket around her neck and went downstairs. As she fingered the locket between her thumb and forefinger, she said, "Thanks, Mom and Dad." It became her favorite piece of jewelry and the envy of Chris and Kelly.

TORNADO
June 9, 1953

WHILE PREPARING MY HUSBAND FRAN'S favorite meal - potato salad - the pungent, sulfuric odor of hard-boiled eggs assaulted my nose. Fake tears rolled down my cheeks as I chopped a white onion, as if there weren't enough legitimate reasons for tears, I thought. I called my sister Joanie and invited her for supper. "Gee, thanks," Joanie said, "I'll take the 5:15 bus, but I'd better close the windows, the wind's blowing like crazy over here."

After I hung up I thought about Joanie's husband's tragic automobile accident a few months ago. After his death Joanie was forced to move into cheaper housing at the Great Brook Valley Apartments. Her daughter Christina, was barely two months old when the accident happened. Before her tragic loss I barely spoke to Joanie. The old wound caused by her marrying the man I was engaged to wed was hard to get over. But now I felt sorry for her. Besides, she had no one to turn to but me.

I looked outside. A yellowish-green color had changed the leaves and the grass to a dark monotone dullness. I finished the potato salad and puttered around the kitchen.

I wiped grease spots off the stove. I dry-mopped the kitchen floor that was already clean.

It was 6:15. I waited.

I walked around the kitchen arms folded, humming *Santa Lucia,* a tune I resorted to while waiting around or just to alleviate boredom. I folded white duck paper napkins in triangle shapes and placed them in the brown butterfly napkin holder on the table. I feather-dusted the filament strings dancing between the spaces of the round fluorescent light fixture. I kept going back to the window. The dark green foliage and grass metamorphosed to powdery green and cast an eerie spell everywhere. I could almost *feel* the color. The bark on the white birch momentarily lost its identity. Slowly, the delicate blades of grass and the perky leaves on the maple adopted chameleon-like traits. In the next instant the sun shone brightly. I thought about Fran. He was usually home from work at Mass Electric by now.

It was 6:45. I waited.

The kitchen door flew open. Fran barged in and asked if I heard about the tornado.

"What?" "Where?"

"Up by Great Brook Valley. Turn on the radio."

"A tornado? We don't have tornadoes around here. Oh, no. Joanie and the baby."

I just did not want to believe it. Even the radio announcer sounded stunned as he continued to relate the grim news. My heart sank when I heard:

"At 5:15 this afternoon a tornado devastated the northern end of our city. All off-duty medical personnel, policemen, firemen and civilian volunteers are asked to report to the disaster area immediately. The National Guard, Civil Defense and the American Red Cross have dispatched rescue teams to the stricken area."

Joanie should be here by now. Maybe she got hung up downtown. Yes, that was it. I looked out the parlor window hoping I would see Joanie and the baby coming up the street.

It was 7:15. I waited.

I panicked when the radio announcer said a baby was killed and scores of passengers were seriously injured, when a 12-ton bus was flung 40 feet and smashed into a building at Great Brook Valley. I looked at Fran in disbelief. This could not happen to Joanie and the baby. Fran nodded toward the door and said, "C'mon, let's see if we can get to Joanie's. She probably never left her house." Just as we were going out the door the phone rang. It must be Joanie, I thought, but it was for Fran. There was a power outage on Lincoln Street and they needed him there. Fran took the Jeep. I took the Chevy. I headed for downtown to check the bus stops en route. Joanie had to transfer to a bus on Main Street to get to my house. There was no sign of Joanie and the baby. I began to pray. I drove away from the downtown area and headed toward Great Brook Valley. Pelting rain splashed on the windshield in sheets. The wipers could barely keep up with the onslaught. Now I knew what zero visibility meant. I was almost there. As I approached Lincoln Plaza the car screeched to a halt and a yellow-slickered policeman flagged me down.

DETOUR.

When I reached the fringe of the tornado-stricken area I could not believe my eyes. The Red Cross, policemen, firemen, National Guardsmen, and scores of civilian volunteers were picking their way through the rubble. Red and amber ambulance lights swirled endlessly while chanting their mournful, wailing sounds. Cruisers roamed defiant over the depressed landscape. When I got out of the car I tripped over bricks and loose wet boards. As I walked my sneakers squished and gushed water through their pores. I dodged assorted pieces of broken glass. Suddenly, I fell and came eye to eye with an injured cat squirming in agony. His pleading eyes and scorched black paws reached out to me, but I got up and kept going. I had to find my sister and the baby. Demolished cars formed grotesque sculptures of cold metal and chrome. Dazed people walked listlessly; bruised, bleeding, and begging for help.

Bodies were sprawled lifeless, where neat brick buildings and saplings barely born had lined the streets. Colorful laundry hung awkwardly from trees like headless scarecrows. I tripped over more broken glass. My sneakers were red with blood. I fell inches from a sizzling cable wire and moved away slowly like a cornered animal and struggled to my feet. An old woman sat motionless on a ladder-back chair, Whistler fashion, where her kitchen must have been. I went to see if I could help her, but when I touched her shoulder she fell over, stiff, apparently dead.

Tacoma Street where Joanie lived was in shambles. I walked right through where the picture window had been and gazed around what was once the living room. A vicious *interior decorator* had come and moved things around.

Remorse set in. I thought about those long months I did not speak to Joanie. How very lonely, how isolated she must have felt. Tears welled up at the thought that I might never have a chance to speak to her again. Joanie's sky-blue and white parakeet lay crushed in its cage - his bulging, black shoe-button eyes staring, lifeless. A roly-poly red and white plastic toy clown stood upright in the midst of the rubble, as though nothing had happened. I walked around aimlessly like a lone piece of deadwood drifting downstream. A Red Cross worker offered me a cup of hot chocolate, but I could not drink it. She walked me back to my car. I headed for home. Sadness fell over me like a heavy black cloak. My heart ached for those who died and for those they left behind. I could not stop thinking about the cat. I wish I had picked it up. He must be dead by now. I cried all the way home. Fran was back. I turned off the ignition and wrapped my arms around the wheel. I did not want to cry anymore. After a few minutes I got out of the car. When I opened the kitchen door I heard Fran on the phone.

"It's City Hospital. Joanie and the baby are okay. Just a few cuts and bruises. They're keeping them overnight."

Fran hugged me and held me close.

"Oh, thank God, thank God, thank you God."

I could not stop crying, but now they were tears of joy and relief.

★★★★★★★

Based on the Worcester, Massachusetts tornado June 9, 1953

NO PLACE LIKE HOME

DURING A VISIT TO MY gynecologist I was advised that a Diagnostic-Curettage (D&C) was necessary and I would be admitted to the hospital as soon as a bed was available. Two weeks passed. I had long since packed my overnight bag and made sure to include Tolstoy's *War and Peace* that never got past chapter one. It was not easy to concentrate on such a book with five kids and one husband clamoring for my attention. At bedtime I would collapse and sleep until the alarm rang at five o'clock. I tried getting up an hour earlier to get in some reading time. I was beat by the third day. I put Tolstoy back on the shelf.

The hospital called. I was told I would be admitted to Ward One. When I got to Admissions the receptionist was on the phone. She paused and said she would be with me in a minute. She was ordering lunch from the deli. Her questions lasted half an hour, but by that time I was so annoyed I thought about going home to pray for a *healing*. The receptionist got a call from Ward One telling her there were no beds available. An emergency came up in the ER and the patient was given my bed.

I was admitted a week later.

A student nurse took my blood pressure as she told me she was new at it. I could tell. I thought I would pass out from the pain. I opened my book. Two minutes later a nurse came in with a pricking instrument and a rubber tube to draw blood. Back to my book. Momentarily I heard footsteps shuffling toward my room. The ward doctor came in to give me the once-over. He said his name was Doctor Habibi and he was from India. After he kneaded my stomach like bread dough he left, assuring me that everything would be *alrite*.

Back to my book? No such luck. A woman visitor in spike heels clickety-clacked by my room. I heard the echo all the way down to the nurse's station. A few minutes later I heard a loud whining noise in the hallway. A cleaning lady was passing the vac. I put the book down and thought about the peace and quiet of my home.

A priest popped and said, "You are going to surgery tomorrow?"

I nodded yes.

"Would you like to confess yourself? It is always good to be prepared at a time like this."

After my confession I thought . . . I had not asked to see a priest. Someone sent him, someone who knew something I did not know. Maybe the doc did not tell me everything. I am not going to pull through this and he knows it. I was so worried I could hardly finish my supper. Soon, the enema nurse came in which added to my anxiety. I swore if they ever got me into a hospital again I would have to be unconscious. I was given a sleeping pill. A while after I tried to pick up my book. It felt like a five-pound dumbell.

Morning rolled around and my doctor explained what he was going to do. I was pricked in the arm to make me drowsy An intern came in with a gurney for my trip to the OR. He told me to roll over on it. What a joke. I could hardy move from being groggy and he expected miracles. It took three husky nurses to do the job.

I was wheeled into a room next to a row of sinks where surgeons were scrubbing up. Their echo-chamber voices floated like wavy sentences around me. I could not help but hear their endless chatter about how many patients they lost. One of them said he did *that operation* five times and they all died. Then this same voice said something to the effect that some surgeons are so mediocre. HA! I tried to laugh in my semi-conscious state, thinking he should have hung up his scalpel long ago. I wondered why such learned men could be so tactless in their conversations, knowing that patients are lying helplessly half-doped waiting to meet the knife. When I was wheeled in for surgery a nurse said, "I'm putting some stockings on you dearie, I just want to let you know what I'm doing."

To which the anesthetist said, "You don't have to tell her what you're doing, she *knows* what you're doing."

My numb lips refused to smile but inside I felt humorous about it. I was given pentothal and told to start counting. Before the count of three I was in *la-la land.* When I returned from the twilight zone I thought . . . Didn't they start me yet? But when I saw the rails on the sides of the bed I knew it was over. It seemed like the anesthesia would never wear off. Someone asked if I wanted coffee or tea. I could not even see who said it let alone hold on to a cup.

When I had all my wits about me I was anxious to leave. Peace and quiet in a hospital? It will never happen. Tolstoy did not have a chance. The doc said I should take it easy for the next couple of weeks. Yay! Now I know I'll finish Tolstoy. And I will never complain about having five kids and one husband underfoot again. There really is NO PLACE LIKE HOME.

****

MUCH ADO ABOUT SOMETHING MADDENING

HONESTLY! YOU WOULD THINK THAT women over age sixty are a breed apart from the younger generation as far as hairstyles go. There are myriad hairstyles to choose from for all age groups, but once you reach sixty-ish you look like a clone of Ann Landers. I have not set foot in a beauty salon for several years because I have given up trying to put my point across. I might as well be talking to a row of shampoo bottles. Once you look like you have joined the ranks of retirees, forget it. Every hairstyle is identical.

I am surprised at the hairdressing industry. You would think they would have caught on by now. Don't they know there are more women over sixty now than ever before in our history? So why not create new and exciting hairstyles for them? There are plenty of us who can afford their services.

Time and again I have been disappointed after having my hair done because of a disinterested operator. When I wanted to look special for a wedding, guess what happened?

Every woman over sixty or so at the reception had a hairstyle just like mine. That's maddening! I realize the beauty industry focuses mainly on youth because that is where lucrative market is but, yoo-hoo, there are many of us over sixty who still have a forever young, forever forty mentality. Isn't it time for the beauty insdustry to get with the program? Many of today's women over sixty are more beauty conscious, more vital, and more *with it* than ever before.

I have repeatedly told beauty operators that I want a hairstyle that fits *me.* I even brought in pictures and sketches of what I would like. Forget it. It is a nightmare out there. Most of the time the operators start chatting with another operator about a previous nights' date. I am not in the least bit interested in what happens in the back seat of a Toyota Corolla.

Once, I distinctly asked not to have any hair cut off at the neck. While leafing through Redbook trusting my request was understood, the operator snipped the neck hair exposing two black moles that came with age. That whole summer I wore a scarf to cover my shame. By the time my hair was long enough for another *do* my hair had turned squirrel gray in back and salt and pepper gray in front. I opted for a color to hide the gray. Big mistake. The hair around my forehead turned snow white, adding ten years to my appearance, and the rest of my hair was carrot orange. I was devastated. In desperation I chopped off all but half an inch of my hair and bought a wig. I lived in fear that a big wind would blow it off at the Plaza. I was sure my hair would grow back to normal in a few months. It took a whole year! I went to a new beauty salon and told an operator my tale of woe. She consulted with the manager who suggested that I go with a softer color. I chose warm sand. To my total dismay my hair turned banana yellow. Back to chop, chop, and back to my wig. I know that wearing a wig too long is not healthy for the scalp, so before I go completely bald will someone please tell the beauty operators to pay attention to the *over sixty* women's requests? I predict that the entrepreneur who gets on the bandwagon first and focuses on women over sixty will rake it in like Flynn. In the meantime, maybe it is time for a gray wave revolution. Dynamic women over sixty, UNITE!

****

THE CAR, THE FOG, AND ME

On a foggy morning in March I went shopping at the Plaza. I browsed around at CVS and bought a few things. As I walked out of the store towards my car I met my friend Freda in the parking lot and we gabbed for about half an hour. She left. The following incident between the car, the fog, and me proved to be an enriching experience. I turned the key. Nothing. I had forgotten to shut the lights off and there I was stuck with a dead battery. I decided then and there to join Triple A first chance I got. I went to the pay phone to call a cab. No cabs available for half an hour. I was about a mile from home. It started to rain. Lucky I had an umbrella in the trunk. I started to walk. At first I felt a little uneasy and awkward. The rain turned to mist then mist to rain.

After a few minutes of mental griping about why this happened to me, I decided to change my attitude and count my blessings. I thanked God that I had a healthy body and a healthy mind. I had a devoted husband, five healthy kids and a roof over my head. Now and then I reached out to catch the warm droplets dripping from the brown celluloid balls on the tips of the gored umbrella. Soon, I began to sense a feeling of calm and inner peace inside me.

I was free to think about anything I wanted for one whole mile. I dry-mopped the floor of my mind and invited the past to come in. I remembered poems, going as far back as the first grade.

> I had a little dog and his name was Ted.
> I put him to sleep in a good warm bed.
> He soon fell asleep and began to snore.
> And woke the little dog that lived next door.

In winter I get up at night, and dress by yellow candle light.
In summer quite the other way, I have to go to bed by day.
I have to go to bed and see, the birds still hopping in the tree,
And hear the grown-up people's feet, still going past me in the street.

I have a little shadow that goes in and out with me,
And what can be the use of him is more than I can see.
He is very, very like me from my heels up to my head,
And I see him jump before me when I jump into my bed.

Time ticked back further still to the month of May, 1931. On my First Communion day, my father carried me the short distance to church because it was raining. He held a big black umbrella that had a shiny wooden cane handle. As we went over the 48-step bridge he took great care that my veil and shoes would not get wet. I felt secure in my father's arms. Such fond memories, I thought. The past kept beckoning. It took me back again to that same month of May. Boys and girls dressed pure white began their procession down the aisle while singing the traditional First Communion hymn:

C'èst le grand jour, bientot l'ange mon frère,
Partagera son banquet avec moi.
Des pleurs de joie humecte ma paupière,
O mon Jésus, je cour, je vol a Toi.

Suddenly, I was in the present as I stepped into a cold puddle. Teary-eyed, I mentally closed the door of the past. As I turned the corner of my street it did not seem as though I had walked a whole mile. I rather hoped it had not ended so soon.

****

NO END TO MADNESS

I JUST KNEW IT WAS going to be one of those days. I awoke to such a racket from the kids fighting over which cartoon they were going to watch that the pounding in my head would make a migraine seem like a pin prick. The TV knob was dying a slow death at the hands of five Saturday morning tube-addicts. I settled the whole matter fairly. I disconnected the TV.

The next worst thing the kids do together is eat. At mealtime Dennis is always at the table first. While the others are wrestling for chairs and banging spoons on the porcelain-top table, he's eenie-meenie-minie-mo-ing the ten boxes of mini-cereal while I contemplate moving to Alaska alone.

My husband Fran gets up and slams the bedroom door and I hear him clearly grouching that it's a rotten shame that a father cannot have at least one day of rest, after working like a dog all week. I feel like yelling through the door, "Hey, big boy, do you realize a mother does not get any rest at all her whole life through until she is resting in peace?"

I tell the kids to clean up, then I clean up after them. I send them outside to play. Whew! I sit down with a cup of coffee to relax. Fran gets up and asks me if his breakfast is ready.

I grumble as I fry bacon, eggs and toast for his majesty.

It starts to rain. Fran looks for his fishing gear. He says they bite better when it is raining. He goes out the door whistling a happy tune as the kids scramble by him to get out of the rain. Fran doesn't even offer to take one of the kids. If that don't beat all!

I decide to let the kids watch TV all day. I make myself a cup of coffee and take out a pile of magazines. Like I said, I just knew it was going to be one of those days. So today, instead doing housework, I am relaxing with my swollen feet on the footstool and reading until his majesty comes home. And he can cook his own fish!

****

NEW IMPROVED

PRACTICALLY EVERY AISLE IN THE food market has some product with a new improved message on the package. For many months now I have been snubbing any product that claims to be new and improved, because I am convinced after using some products that certain manufacturers have not improved anything. My reasoning tells me the quality of many items have been reduced to cut cost. Shame on you, whoever you are. I'm wise to your tricks. So I by-pass every sign that boasts *New Improved.*

Take the most famous round crackers that rhyme with *blitz* as an example. Their new improved flimsy see-through wrapper that is supposed to insure freshness, keeps them so fresh they fall on the counter top in little bitty crumbs. Did you ever try to put peanut butter on crumbs? They hug the knife! It should come as no surprise to you that I have switched to the other brand that rhymes with *brown mouse.* Another item I do not buy anymore since the advent of new improved, is the scouring cleanser that rhymes with *hutch.* The original product my mother used was far better, and it did not cause her to atchoo all over the tub.

I refuse to buy cereal boxes with neat looking zipper openings that rip sideways and off in a little piece between my thumb and forefinger. Those make me so crabby I could spit. And just try to open the bag inside. It feels like it is welded with epoxy glue.

Some toilet tissue manufacturers have got a nerve. They have come out with new improved claims too. HA! The cardboard roll that holds the tissue has been enlarged to almost twice its previous size leaving less paper on the roll. I swear those companies have special agents sitting on toilets in their labs, testing to see how fast the paper flies off the roll and lands on the floor, using twice as much as anyone really needs. Well, they are not fooling me. I just know there is something going on in their labs all to fool the consumer.

It is all about the almighty buck isn't it? Well, I do not care if it takes me an extra half-hour to shop. I check everything. I even carry a ruler that I measure the toilet paper hole with. The managers must think I am a store detective checking out their products so I can report anything fishy going on.

Listen manufacturers, I am sick and tired of crackers that metamorphose into crumbs, cleansers that throw my olfactory center into a tizzy, boxes that rip instead of zip, and toilet tissue rolls with more hole than paper. If you claim to improve your products then IMPROVE THEM! Don't go *hypocriting* around and think we are all dumbells falling for your *shenanigans.* You know who you are. Shame, shame, puddin' tame, everybody knows your "GAME." I just want you to know that I have passed the word around to all my female friends and relatives. We refuse to be your guinea piglets anymore! GET THAT?

★★★★★★★

FELLOW FAT FIGHTERS, REPENT!

ONE MORNING AS I LOOKED at my fat form in the mirror I was filled with disgust and ashamed of myself for giving in to the sin of gluttony. At five-feet seven with a medium frame, weighing 160 pounds and climbing I knew I would soon be shopping at Lane Bryant's. I was in a very tight twelve. Luckily, my excess weight had settled around my middle and my hips so my bulges were easy to hide. And since my family and friends kept telling me I looked great and that I did not need to lose weight, who was I to doubt them? I knew I was in deep trouble however, when my clothes began to choke me. I graduated to a size 14. It got to a point where I could not zip my jeans closed so I tied a shoelace in the buttonhole and twirled it around the button on the other side. I wore overblouses so no one could see the open vee shape underneath it all. I purposely undressed in the dark so my husband would not see what that *dainty little flower* he married had turned into. Totally disgusted with my shape I decided to try to curb my appetite. Since Monday is my *turn a new leaf day* I vowed that things were going to change, but by lunch time my good intentions went awry and I slid back into overeating.

I read somewhere that you should always pig-out the day before you start a diet.

So, the following Sunday my husband and I pigged out at Friendly's, McDonald's, and Papa Gino's. Now I was really ready to get serious about losing weight. I will have this weight problem licked in no time. Sure. Again I had great intentions in the morning, but by supper time it was over. What to do? Oh, I saw all those commercials on TV about diet programs that transform you into a twig in two weeks. One diet program urges fat people to never go on a diet, yet they go on to praise their program that is nothing but another diet.

One day while watching *The Bold and the Beautiful* I wolfed down a scrumptious salami and cheese on rye, inhaled half a bag of Lay's potato chips, and washed it down with a mug of Miller Lite. Another diet commercial came on showing a beautiful slim figure of a young woman who once weighed 200 pounds. She was now into a size 2, thanks to Weight Watchers. Moss green with envy, I signed up at Weight Watchers the next day.

During the first meeting I envisioned myself pulling a little red wagon a la Oprah Winfrey, with 20 pounds of fat trailing behind me and gone forever. I followed the diet religiously. I did not miss one meeting. Once, during a blizzard, I braved the elements in my old Chevy and slid side-saddle all the way. When I arrived the doors were locked. I was the only one who had ventured out in such treacherous weather. I went straight home and did some ironing. Then I dancercized to *Blue Suede Shoes* and other Elvis songs until I worked up a sweat. Between dieting and dancing I should shake off the fat in no time. I continued to go to the weekly meetings.

Gradually, the pounds melted off. I reached my goal in 4 months. I whittled down to a size 10. I was extatic! My sinful ways were behind me at last. As a reward for my incredible achievement I bought myself a green leather jacket. I maintained my weight for 6 months.

Then the demon angel tempted me. I decided I could do this myself. It was all downhill after that. The guardian angel on my right shoulder warned me not to take that extra helping or I would be sorry, but the demon angel on my left shoulder said to go ahead and take it. I listened to the demon angel. And here is the rest of the story.

You guessed it. The pounds came creeping back when my husband and I began to go the fast food route. Before I knew it I had gained all the weight back, plus. My green leather jacket did not fit anymore. I was too embarrassed to go back to Weight Watchers. But one day I braced myself and took the plunge again. My leader greeted me with open arms. I was forgiven. I had fallen by the wayside, or more by the way of Burger King, Big Boy's and Crown Bakery.

Happily, I am on my way to reaching my goal weight once again, and I am determined to attend the meetings once a week without fail. That is the secret. Touching base once a week is the most important factor to losing weight through the Weight Watcher's Plan. Being there it *the* great motivator. You must do it diligently, for your health and for your self-esteem. There is no other way. My favorite fridge magnets read:

THOU SHALT NOT WEIGH MORE THAN THY REFRIDGERATOR!

GLUTTONY IS THE SOURCE OF ALL OUR INFIRMITIES.

****

SCIENCE FAIR UNFAIRNESS

THE PERIOD OF TIME BETWEEN getting up and seeing the kids off to school is nothing short of madness, but on the day their Science Fair projects are due I need the courage of a Joan of Arc. One morning when I had just closed the door the bell rang. Did you ever try to listen to five kids talking frantically two decibels above normal all at the same time?

"Our science projects," yelled Larry, "we have to bring them today."

At the same time Brenda whined, "It's raining Ma, you have to take us."

Dennis said, "Maybe I'll win first prize."

Charlotte quipped, "HA! I'll bet Woofy wins first prize like he does every year."

Stevie, who was already outdoors yelled, "Hurry up Ma, we're gonna be late!"

When we got to school Dennis splashed through a puddle while guarding his poster with his life. Brenda was bawling because one of her Big Dipper stars unglued from her poster and floated in a puddle. You would think it was swishing down the Grand Rapids. Larry got shook up because he was not out of the car yet and the bell was ringing. As I waved goodbye I yelled, "I hope you all win a prize." I knew very well they were not going to win any prizes.

The kids who would win prizes - guaranteed - were those whose parents helped them, or those whose parents did the projects with little input from the kids, or those whose fathers were specialists in some field. Take Woofy, whose father is a big-wig in a missiles plant. It is obvious that Woofy's sophisticated projects are not the brain-child of a little kid.

I thought about how my kids spent a whole month doing research and worked tediously on their projects, and that the finished work was the result of their efforts alone. Parental input involved buying supplies, period.

When the kids got home I knew by their long faces they did not win any prizes.

Dennis said, "Woofy won first prize."

"Yah." Echoed Brenda. "Why can't Daddy help us like Woofy's father does?"

Charlotte complained, "Daddy's just a plain ol' carpenter."

"Sh-h-h," I said, "here comes Dad now."

"Hi, Dad." The kids chirped as he walked in.

My husband, quick to pick that something was amiss said, "Okay, what's up?"

After I told him the story he decided that next year he is going to help the kids with their science projects. I asked if he had anything in mind.

"Yup." He said. "Mechanics Illustrated sells Lie Detector Kits. I'll put one together and one of the kids can test it on all the kids who take part in the Science Fair.

H-m-m-m. I can't imagine what the first question will be.

****

TABLE TALK

UNFORTUNATELY, DOCTOR SPOCK CAME ALONG during the years when I did not have time to read. I am sure the Doc had good advice on how to cope with kids bickering at the table. Five kids wrestling with a box of cornflakes is pretty nerve-wracking, and the dialogue, Oh, my!

BREAKFAST:

"Pass the sugar."

"Push over."

"Ma, Charlotte's kicking me on purpose."

"Pass the sugar."

"Ma, Brenda's gawking at me."

"Ma, Larry's slurping his cereal like pig."

"Ma, Stevie dumped all the sugar in his cereal and he knew I wanted some."

"Ma, Ma, Ma." Did you ever hear a kid say "Pa?"

LUNCH:

"Ma, Stevie was choking me to death on the way to school."

"Ma, Larry got punished for giving Woofy Haratoonian a bloody nose."

"Ma, Miss Callahan said if Charlotte doesn't stop yakking in class she's going to get kicked out of school."

"Ma, Dennis threw his report card in the sewer and almost fell in."

"Ma, I think Brenda got kidnapped, she wasn't in the lines."

Enter Brenda. "Ma, Mr. O'Brien kept me after class just because I called him "Hey, Obee."

SUPPER:

Pa asks, "How was school today kids?"

Like perfect little angels they all answer in well-modulated voices, as I marvel that these are the same kids who sat at this very table just a few hours ago. Know what? In my next life I want to come back as "Pa."

****

THE NERVE OF SOME MEN

I DON'T KNOW WHERE SOME men get the audacity to talk about women drivers. The minute they get behind the wheel they think they own the whole pavement. The other day a man driver had the nerve to try to pass me on the right, which is illegal in our state. Presently, I tooted the horn to get his attention and he had the gall to make a face at me and started waving his hands and yelling. I could read his lips uttering obscenities. When I mimicked him by waving my arms in the same manner (minus obscenities) zap went the panic button and he zoomed out of sight just missing my fender by one *nth*. While trying to get my composure, another man driver blasted his horn for me to get out of his way. I did. I decided thereafter to give men drivers the right of way or risk getting hung up on a telephone pole. My husband would have no pity on me if such a thing happened, because he feels the same way about women drivers as other men do.

Did you ever get caught going the wrong way on a one way street? I know people do this but did you ever get caught I mean, by a traffic cop? I did. Now, if it had been a man, the cop would have waved him on and said, "Oh that's all right, we all make mistakes." But no, it was me, and the cop was not even near my car yet and he was yelling and growling.

Mini-bubbles of sweat danced on my forehead. There he stood, with knobby fists planted firmly on his size forty-eight hips yelling at me. There is nothing that embarrasses me more than a yelling cop. My first ticket. I was crushed. It's at a time like this I wish I had listened to my aunt the nun in Canada and joined the Cloisterettes.

"Wouldn't you know it would be a woman. Didn't you see that sign over there?" A pack of nosy people gathered to watch me squirm. Through tear-filled eyes and quivering voice I tried to explain that I was late for school and . . . The grouch wrote me up and ordered me to take a left. I obeyed, secretly wishing I would run over his big feet. As I made the turn I saw another car behind me in the same predicament. It was a man driver, and would you believe the cop smiled at him and waved him on? See what I mean? I wrote the following verse to express my feelings.

NON-COMPASSIONED OFFICER

He was fat and grumpy Lord
The policeman on the beat.
He made some accusations
As I sunk low in my seat.
I was on my way to school,
It was getting late you see.
Prayed not to get a ticket,
But he didn't pity me.
I couldn't understand it,
Til a sign my eyes did meet.
My Chevy went the wrong way,
On a lousy one way street.

Pungent Prayer Mediapolis News 1977

****

THE CHASE

HAVING A BABY WAS TO be a brand new experience for Donna and Fran. As the months passed Donna became more and more concerned about Fran's nervousness at Expectant Parents classes. Yet, all the while he kept insisting that the whole thing was going to be a cinch. One night after classes Donna said, "You'll never hack it Fran. You get queasy at the sight of catchup on TV commercials. You'll probably pass out on the spot."

"Now, don't you fret your pretty little head about me," Fran asserted, "I can take anything. There's no need to get excited and nervous about a natural thing like having a baby."

The ninth month came around and Donna wondered every night if this would be *it*. Then on a hot August night it was *it*. Donna shook Fran out of a sound sleep. Fran jumped out of bed like a bolt of lightning and said, "Oh, no. Are you okay? Is it now? Holy Moley. W-what t-time is it?"

"It's 2:30. Hurry. The pains are getting closer and closer."

Fran panicked.

"Did you see the car keys anywhere? Oh, no, I think I left them in the car."

"Holy Moley, the car doors are locked. We'll have to call a cab."

Donna's water broke. Fran paced back and forth like a tiger looking for a means of escape.

Donna said, "Hey, are you going to the hospital in your PJ's?"

Fran put his cut-down jeans on backward. When he took them off to put them on right the car keys fell on the floor. Then he couldn't find his sneakers. As he knelt down to look under the bed he hit his head on the open drawer of the night stand and cussed a few choice words.

"Hurry up, Fran, I just might have the baby right here."

Fran, still on his knees said, "Hey, like I said, there's no need to get excited and nervous about a natural thing like having a baby." Nervously, Fran put his sneakers on, left them untied and said, "Hurry up and get in the car."

They zoomed away at 60 miles an hour, up down and around corners trying to make time on the five-mile trip to St. V's.

"It won't be long now Hon." Fran said in a reassuring tone.

Suddenly, a police cruiser hot on their trail caused Fran to screech to a halt.

A big burly officer yelled, "And where the hell do you think you're going Mack? This is a 30-mile zone. Are you crazy?"

Fran, wide-eyed and tight-lipped, looking like he had swallowed a bug, pointed to Donna's abdomen as she squirmed in the throes of a contraction.

"Follow me!" Instructed the officer.

Cambridge Street was bright with flashing blue lights of cruisers parked horizontally across the road.

ROADBLOCK.

The officer turned around and Fran followed.

At the Kelley Square intersection Fran beeped the horn and waved for the officer to stop.

OUT OF GAS.

Donna waddled like a duck toward the cruiser, supporting her beach-ball belly with taut, outstretched fingers. Fran followed nervously behind her. Big beads of sweat rolled down Fran's face. The piercing siren broke the eerie quiet that lurked on the night shift at St. V's.

The skeleton crews' heads turned in unison as the doors flew open. The officer carried Donna in, she, in her mother's size forty-four flimsy nightgown, and Fran, looked totally distraught and ready to be admitted himself. A nurse dashed over with a wheelchair and a stream of questions followed. As Donna moaned and groaned, Fran tried to answer the questions.

"Did you call your doctor?"

"N-no."

"What's your doctor's name?"

"Uh, M-Murphy. Doctor M-Murphy."

"What's your wife's name?"

"Uh, D-Donna, yah, that's it."

"What's your name?"

"W-Who me? Uh, O'Brien, no F-Fran, I mean uh."

"Insurance?"

"Oh, yah, h-here's the card."

"This is your Visa card. I need your insurance ID."

"Did your water break yet honey?"

"Yes, about half an hour ago."

A nurse grabbed the wheel chair and sped away with Fran trailing behind. W-H-A-C-K!

The swinging doors connected with Fran's nose. As Donna turned around to look for Fran, she spotted him in a wheelchair being told by a nurse to stop being such a big baby. "Just put your head down between your knees and pinch your nose. It's only a nosebleed for God's sake, you're not exactly at death's door."

Fran heard Donna plead from afar, "C'mon Fran, you're supposed to help me breath and count."

Three nurses positioned Donna on a gurney, and after a quick check on her progress one of them said, "No time to prep her, she's ready. Keep your legs together honey, and don't push!"

Minutes later, the baby was born, minus Doctor Murphy who was on vacation, no breathing and counting excercises, and no Fran. Momentarily, Fran, all bent out of shape, staggered into the delivery room, looked at Donna and the baby, and just above a whisper he managed to say, "Holy-Moley!" Then he passed out cold on the floor.

****

SUMMER MADNESS WITH A FRINGE BENEFIT

SCHOOL'S OUT. GINA'S FRUMPY LEICESTER High sweatshirt and dirty gym sneakers, smelly from being holed-up in her locker, land on the shiny red plastic bean bag chair in her bedroom, better known as a disaster area to her Mom, Dad, and 8-year-old brother Kevin. A Pass At Your Own Risk crude plywood sign hangs lopsided from an old black shoelace on the door. Over Gina's bed masking tape secures mini-posters of Jean-Claude Van Damme, Mel Gibson, and the Rock Groups, AeroSmith, and Duran-Duran. Gina plops down on her full-sized bed, the side that isn't littered with a big boom box, issues of Seventeen and Worcester Magazine. A half-empty bag of stale Dorito's and a large stuffed brown shaggy dog adds to the mess on the jade green comforter. Hands joined behind her head, feet crossed, Gina thinks about summer and the freedom it would bring. The only down side to vacation is that both Gina's parents have full-time jobs, and Gina has to baby-sit her bratty little brother. You name it, Kevin's been there, done that. Besides being a little hellion at home, he embarrasses Gina every chance he gets. She hates to take him anywhere, especially food shopping. While chewing a wad of cherry bubble gum Gina dials her friend Kim, pops a bubble and says, "Hi Kim, wanna go to the Big Y?'

Maybe we'll see that cool dude Ricky Jordan. He worked there last summer. I heard him talking to Sheila and Madeline last day of school. He's going to work there again this summer. I think he works in produce now. He used to be a bagger, remember? I think he got promoted. I saw him once behind the service desk, ya know, where they sell lottery tickets and videos. I guess he moves around a lot." Gina pops another bubble and says, "Hey Kim, can you hear me? I just popped a bubble and it landed on the mouthpiece, the part where I'm talking, ya know, where all the little black holes are? You can hardly hear me?" Gina yelled into the mouthpiece. "See ya at the Big Y around three, okay?"

CRASH! SLAM! BANG!

Gina bolted out of her room. Kevin had roller-bladed down the hall and knocked down everything in his path, landed butt first, and screamed for Gina to help him get up. "You little scuzzball nerd, you scared me to death! Pick that stuff up and move it, we're going to the Big Y. Ma wants hamburg for supper."

Gina, Kim, and Kevin headed for the produce aisle. Ricky was putting tomatoes in the display bin. Kevin wandered off. When they were almost there Gina said, "Check the bod. That's the most gorgeous blue-eyed dude I've ever seen. Think he'd ever give me a tumble?" Gina asked.

"In your dreams." Kim said. "He goes for classy chicks like Sheila and Madeline. Why in the world would he even look at you? You're not exactly Queen of the Nile, ya know."

"Well, you're not exactly a fashion model either." Gina snapped.

Kim shot back. "So what about you, you're always in your grubbies, you chew gum like a camel, and you wear those grungy black sneakers."

"You should talk. You don't even wear socks." Gina snipped.

They moved a little closer to the produce aisle and hid behind a six-foot ficus tree so they could gawk at Ricky without being noticed. Just then they spotted Kevin near the end of the aisle pouncing on the mangos, kiwi fruit, and the purple plums. When a pile of plums toppled to the floor Ricky yelled, "Hey kid. Cut that out. Where's your mother?"

"She ain't here, she works. I'm here with my sister Gina. She thinks you're cute. Oh, here she comes now." Kevin said.

Totally frazzled, Gina picked up the plums and placed them back in the bin, then grabbed Kevin by the neck and the trio headed for the meat case. After she picked a package of hamburg Gina asked Kim, "Hey, where's Kevin?"

"I dunno," Kim said, "he was here a minute ago."

Just then music faded from the sound system and a Julia Child voice blurted, "There's a little boy at the service desk who says his sister Gina is lost. He's wearing a Hulk Hogan tee-shirt, and he's eating a Hershey candy bar. Will Gina please come to the service desk?"

"That kid is going to get it from me now, I warned him he'd better stay with us." Gina said.

And like a raging bull Gina charged toward the service desk with Kim following her. Gina yanked Kevin away and shook him back and forth by the shoulders until he started to cry. All eyes were on Gina as if she was guilty of child abuse, and sheepishly she let go of him and headed for the express aisle. Kevin climbed on the chrome bars and started to do gymnstics and accidentally kicked the lady in front of them. Gina grabbed Kevin by the tail end of his shirt and told him to stop doing that. While Gina and Kim gabbed Kevin disappeared again. Kim found him at the end of the dairy aisle scooping up Ritz crackers as soon as the white-aproned lady put cheese squares on them. Gina paid for the hamburg and the candy bar and they left. After Gina dropped Kim off she yelled at Kevin non-stop all the way home. When their mother got home Gina squealed on Kevin who denied everything.

The whole thing was fluffed off because their mother didn't know who to believe. When their mother was out of ear-shot, Kevin put his thumbs in his ears, waved his fingers up and down and said, "Ha-Ha."

Next shopping day came around too soon for Gina. While she cleaned up the kitchen, Kevin barged in and asked what time they were going to the Big Y. "In a little while." Gina answered. Kevin parked himself in front of the TV.

Two minutes later he asked, "Aren't you ready yet?"

"No, I'm not. Go outside. I still have things to do."

Ding, ding, ding. Kevin kept his finger on the doorbell. Gina grabbed Kevin briskly by the arm and told him to wait in the car. "You give me a pain." Kevin said, as he shook himself away from Gina's grip. "I'm tellin' Ma you're always pickin' on me."

As usual the trio headed for the produce aisle where Ricky was talking with Sheila and Madeline. They were dressed in tight Calvin Klein jeans, skimpy halter tops, and meticulous French braids. Gina was envious of the attention Ricky showered on them. They continued shopping.

That night before going to bed, Gina took a good look at herself in the mirror and no longer wondered why Ricky wouldn't give her a second look. She sat up in bed and leafed through magazines, and visualized Sheila and Madeline, envying them and wishing she could look like them. She picked up the Worcester Magazine and browsed through it. A large ad hit her in the face. *LA FEMINA MODELING AND FINISHING SCHOOL.* Wow! Gina thought. This is really cool. That's it. That's what I'm going to do with my baby-sitting money. She called Kim and asked her if she wanted to sign up with her in September. Kim agreed. After Gina hung up she looked in the mirror again. Her complexion was greasy, her eyes dull, her lips chapped, her hair hadn't seen a shampoo bottle in days, and her posture left something to be desired.

Summer vacation was over. Gina and Kim looked forward to La Femina classes. The first class was an overview of the 20-week course. After discussing their goals and aspirations, each student had a skin analysis. The following week they learned about skin care, poise, posture, and confidence. In the ensuing months they learned about make-up, attaining an ideal figure, hair care and styling, how to act in social situations, and runway techniques a la Miss America. They also learned about fashion awareness, fashion show modeling, personality, public speaking, and voice training. At the end of the course they were completely transformed, and beamed from ear to ear as they walked the walk in LA FEMINA'S Fashion show.

Weekly trips to the BigY became more bearable for Gina and Kim. Instead of getting riled about Kevin, they kept their cool. Next shopping day, they didn't see Ricky. They found out at the service desk that he was off to college, but he would be back next summer. Gina's first thought was that some cute chick would snap him up for sure.

Sumertime. One afternoon Gina, Kim and Kevin went on their usual shopping trip. Kevin was still a pain in the neck, but Gina and Kim ignored him. Their main concern was their appearance and what effect their new look would have on Ricky. They walked around poised and confident. Their meticulous French braids, tight Calvin Klein jeans, and sexy candy-pink tank tops caused all the dudes to do double-takes. Anxious to have Ricky see them, they sashayed over in their runway strut to impress him. And there he was, drop dead gorgeous, placing red apples in the fruit bin.

Ricky looked at Gina and said, "Hi there, doll-face."

"Hi yourself." Gina quipped, giving him a flirtatious wink.

"Hey, it's time for my break." Ricky said. "How about a Coke?"

"Cool." Gina said.

Kim was envious as all-get-out. Sheila and Madeline gaped in disbelief.

And Kevin showed up and said, "I'm tellin' Ma you're flirtin' with all the guys in the market."

To which Gina remarked, "Ask me if I care."

Gina's complete change from a sloppy dresser to a neat looking teenager rubbed off on the care of her bedroom also. She planned to use her next baby-sitting money to fix up her bedroom with the best of everything from Bed & Bath. Her parents were amazed at the complete transformation they saw in Gina. And despite the frustrating times spent at the Big Y with Kevin, it was all worth it to Gina, who never dreamed that the summer that began with *madness* would end up having a *fringe benefit.*

★★★★★★★

TEALEAVES

WHEN MÉMÉ PICARD LEFT NOVA Scotia to spend the summer with my Aunt Isabel down the street, Granny Ross had reservations. Mother and my little sister and I were all Granny had since Grandpa died. We lived in Kerry, New Hamshire, in a four-room cold-water flat in the poor section of town. Mémé arrived on Sunday morning, just in time for the seven o'clock Mass. Mother and my sister and I walked to Aunt Isabel's and after Mémé greeted us with hugs and kisses she asked, "Where's Granny?"

"Oh, she's got injeshun, she ain't goin' t'church." My sister said.

Granny had not missed Mass in years. She really had to be sick to miss Mass, but by late afternoon she felt a little better and we all went to Aunt Isabel's to play cards. Mémé and Granny locked horns during a game of Rummy. "Those aren't the rules." Mémé griped, "I'm not playing with you again unless we do it my way." Pointing to Granny Mémé said, "You'd better go to confession before next Sunday or you can't receive communion. It's a mortal sin to miss Sunday Mass, you know."

As we left Aunt Isabel's, Granny paused to look at Mémé's wedding picture on the buffet in the parlor, a picture of sweet innocence, she thought. Look who's talking about mortal sins. Granny thought about the time she and Mémé were dating young boys in Kerry. She remembered one particular night when Mémé went off in nearby woods with a boy. Mémé was mad because Granny would not go with them with her date. Mémé was the daring one who would do anything for a good time, and Granny soon parted company with her because Mémé had a reputation for being wild.

Granny's favorite pastime, reading tea leaves, often revealed scary things like the day she saw the shape of a crow (an omen of death) in her teacup. Our downstairs neighbor, Mr. Martin, got into a car accident and died. Another time when Granny saw tea leaves scatterred all over her cup, she predicted that a widespread disaster was near. Soon, an epidemic of influenza ravaged the northeast. Before Mémé arrived, Granny knew trouble was afoot when she saw tea leaves all around the edge of her cup. Mémé arrived the following week.

Granny's day began at 5 o'clock. She shuffled across the faded red and gray linoleum, bent over, tsst, tsst, tsst, tsst, in her peacock-blue felt slippers. With each step the black leather tips peeked out from under her long paisely-print apron that skimmed the floor. She boiled water for tea.

In one pocket of her apron Granny had a red railroad handkerchief and a shiny round ebony snuff box decorated with red and gold oriental designs. Moist dark tobacco, the color of sifted, rich dark loam, smelled like teaberry gum whenever Granny opened her *tabatière* for a pinch of snuff. In her other apron pocket she had some white Canada Peppermints, and often times she would put her soiled handkerchief in the wrong pocket. Result: white and brown peppermints! We pretended to put the mints in our mouths but threw them away in the waste basket when Granny wasn't looking.

Granny spent hours in the old rocker by the Glenwood stove in the kitchen.

When she was not knitting or mending, she was cutting squares out of old dresses for the next patchwork quilt. Since she was illiterate, Granny enjoyed listening to my mother read to her.

She looked forward to hearing the love story *Recambole* serialized in the *Kerry Times*. But she especially liked listening to passages from the New Testament in French.

My sister and I looked forward to visiting Aunt Isabel's especially when Mémé was visiting. Mémé was adept at knitting and canning. That summer she put up 20 quarts each of tomatoes, bread and butter pickles, and piccalilli. When Aunt Isabel told Mémé that Granny loved piccalilli, Mémé thought . . . that bickering old flea bag isn't getting any piccalilli from me.

During canning season spicy smells saturated Aunt Isabel's kitchen. We could smell the strong odors of cinnamon cloves, celery seed, mustard seed, peppercorns, onions, and vinegar as my sister and I approached her house. We went there almost every day to get the jars ready for sterilizing, and to help around the kitchen. As a reward, Mémé made yummy divinity fudge that melted in our mouths.

When Mémé finished canning the piccalilli, she squeezed the juice out of the ecru muslin bag that held the smelly spices and gave it to us to take home. When Granny looked at the bag she pursed her lips and scoffed, "Hmmph!" As she picked up speed on her rocking chair, her knitting needles followed suit. We put the bag in a bowl on the table and it smelled up the whole kitchen.

On the days we went to Aunt Isabel's Granny hardly spoke to us when we got home. She was visibly annoyed that Aunt Isabel had us over there so often. But on the days we did not go there Granny was elated. She would sing Scottish songs while we shuffled our feet and pretended to step-dance to the jig-like tunes. When she made taffy we got our hands all gooey pulling the buttery candy firm. Making taffy became a weekly pastime even though we had mayonnaise jars full of it in the pantry.

When we were finished we were too tired to go to Aunt Isabel's. Granny liked that. We took turns holding skeins of yarn around our wrists, and swayed our arms back and forth as Granny rolled the yarn into a ball. Her days revolved around us.

Soon after canning season Mémé took to her knitting. One day she couldn't find her needles and on a rare visit to Granny's she asked if she could borrow a pair of hers. Granny, who did not want to seem selfish in front of us, obliged. After a long while Granny began to wonder why Mémé had not returned the needles, and she decided to go get them. Mémé faked that she lost them. Granny was furious. "You're lying," Granny growled, "those were my mother's and I want them back right now."

"I told you I lost them." Mémé said.

Seething with anger Granny said, "I'm telling the priest about you, then he'll see you for what you *really* are."

Mémé's thoughts flashed back to that night in the woods and she feared Granny would tell the priest about her shady past. "Oh, well, if that's the way you feel about it." Mémé said.

One day Mémé chatted over the fence with a new neighbor. The newcomer was fishing for gossip about people in town. She had already been to some sewing circles, and found out from other tongue-waggers about the scandal that rocked the town many years ago. An aborted baby's remains were found in a trash can in the town common. The young girl in question fled to Nova Scotia. "I heard Granny Ross knows who it is," the neighbor said, "but they say the religious old twit swore on the Bible she would never tell. Imagine that!" Mémé was upset about what the gossip said. She was confident that Granny would never tell, but it was in Mémé's best interest to stay on Granny's good side. Mémé even brought over some piccalilli. Sometimes she would help Granny cut material for patchwork quilts. On one such occasion Mémé asked Granny to read her tea leaves.

As Granny held the warm cup in both hands she saw a diagonal row of tea leaves from the bottom to the top of the cup.

"You're going on a trip - far away." Granny said. "It seems like you're running away from something."

Union Station. The giant wheels squeaked slowly to a stop on the shiny steel gray tracks. My mother, Aunt Isabel, and my sister and I hugged Mémé, while Granny sniffed some snuff. As the train pulled away, we all waved goodbye. My sister and I cried. Our Granny sighed.

★★★★★★★

MEMORIES OF A CHRISTMAS PAST

WHEN I WAS A KID, we were poor. There was me, known as Jackie the tomboy, Jenny, my 5-year-old sister, and Pa and Ma. We lived in a six-room cold-water flat by the railroad tracks in a small New England town. On a dreary October morning in 1929, I left my beat-up wooden wagon with its wobbly red scooter wheels outside the door at Nick's Spa, where I picked up the Daily Post to deliver before school. The brass bell dangling from the cold door knob jingled as I opened the dark gray wooden door. Inside, the smell of coffee perkin', eggs fryin', and bacon sizzlin', made me feel good all over. Not that I was hungry or anythin', I'd just had breakfast - oatmeal and toast - same's every other mornin'.

When Pa was too sick to work at the barber shop, he'd fix shoes at home to earn extra money. Ma took in washing and mending from the rich folks across town, so's she could help Pa a little. Me, I only wanted to sell papers and save money to buy a new wagon like the one I saw at Letourneau's hardware store. It cost 10 dollars. Oh, how I wanted that wagon. I wanted it so bad I stopped buying licorice sticks for a penny like I used to every mornin' at Nick's, one for me and one for Jenny.

I passed the penny candy case real quick and went outside. Big bold letters stared me in the face as I untied the paper bundle.

STOCK MARKET CRASHES!

Didn't sound important to me. I was twelve years old, and they were jus' words, same's any other headline, I thought. 'Sides, it didn't matter to me anyhow what the words meant, 'long as I could make money to buy the wagon.

That afternoon I stopped at Letourneau's like I did every day after school. As I clutched my books under one arm, I cupped my other hand over my eyes so's I could see better. Jus' then the sun broke through the clouds and the wagon seemed to disappear. I headed home. As I skipped gingerly down Canterbury street, I could feel the cold cement sidewalk through the holes in my shoes. 'least I had warm mittens and a hat and scarf. My long black cotton stockings kept my legs and feet warm, 'til the soles of my black high-laced *bottines* wore out, that is. Right now it felt like the holes were the size of a quarter. I hoped Pa wouldn't be too tired to fix them tonight. Just then my thoughts switched to the beef stew and dumplings we were having for supper, last night's leftovers.

When I opened the kitchen door, I couldn't smell the stew and the table wasn't set. The shades were down and all was real quiet. I felt kinda funny. I closed the door slowly. Ma came out of the parlor snifflin' and wipin' her eyes with the corner of her apron. Jenny tagged along half behind her. Ma could hardly talk. Pa was dead. We all sat on the dull green mohair sofa and cried for a long, long time. What would we ever do without Pa? After the the funeral Ma said I'd have to help out with the money I earned from my paper route. I'd have to pay for the food we bought on credit at Lavallee's last week. The money I saved for the wagon would go for part of next month's rent. Pa had no insurance, so there was no money at all. I didn't want to use the money I had saved for the wagon. I was mad. Why did Pa have to die?

Why did we have to be so poor? It wasn't fair. Nothing was fair. I gave Ma the money grudgingly. Now, I'd have to look for another job if I wanted to buy the wagon. But how could I find work when so many grownups were loafing? I prayed for snow so's I could earn money shovelin' like last winter when I did old lady Lamothe's walk for ten cents a snowstorm, only this year I'd charge her more, and Mrs. Vandal too. I tried to get new customers for the Post. No luck. I asked Mr. Lavallee if I could do odd jobs for him around the store. No luck. One Saturday afternoon I went to the shoe factory on the other side of the bridge to look for a job. The man in charge looked at me and laughed like a hyena an said I couldn't punch my way out of a paper bag. Besides he didn't give jobs to girls. I was so mad I wanted to spit. I said, "I can work. They don't call me tomboy for nothin,' jus' hire me and you'll see." After thinking about it the man hired me, but he said he could only pay me five cents a day. I would have to sweep all the floors and do other odd jobs every day after school. I skipped home, jumped the bridge two steps at a time to tell Ma about the job. A week passed. On pay-day, the boss, chewing on a wet brown cigar handed me a nickel. "B-but, Mista, I thought it was five cents a day."

"For the sloppy work you did. G'wan, get outa here, ya dumb kid."

I left the factory feeling bitter at the whole world. I'll never get that wagon now. One day after school I crossed Crystal Park and went to some stores on Main Street hoping I'd find a job. Nobody was hiring.

Dusk. I didn't want to go home. I wanted to cry. When I got to the middle of the bridge I heard the haunting whistle of a train in the distance. It made me sad. I watched the train come from a quiet tiny speck far away to a roaring, grumbling noise mixed with smoke coughing from the black funnel of the smokestack. I closed my eyes and held my breath. I felt smothered by the smoke and shaken by the vibration of the crude wooden boards under my feet. I didn't care if I was full of soot. I didn't care about anything at all. Snow began to fall.

I stayed there until the tracks and everything around me was covered with a shiny white powdery dusting. I headed for home. When I reached the other side of the bridge the ground glistened as though a thousand magic wands had touched down to make the earth twinkle. As I walked I felt a circle of numbing cold press through the holes in my shoes, and my feet began to ache. Oh, what of it, I thought. It wasn't easy for Ma either. Her back hurt her sometimes at night from bending over the sewing she had to do. Oh, she never said her back hurt, but I could tell it did by the way she rubbed it when she was stirring somehing on the stove. I forgot about my aching feet as I made fresh imprints in the new-fallen snow.

When I got home Ma said I'd have to stand in the bread lines at church. I went the next day. I saw some sad sights all around me. Slowly, I began to understand what the grownups meant by *hard times.* There was poor Joe Belanger, hungry and looking for a handout. 'Long as I could remember he always wore the same old raggy clothes. I wondered what kept him from freezing to death in winter. Maybe all those people standing around kept the wind off him. And Farley, the town drunk, looking pleased that someone else was sharing his misery. Hobos who rode the rails were part of the line-up too. But the strangest of all was Mr. Epstein still wearing his banking clothes and those gray things half over his shoes. As I stood in those lines with my old wagon, I'd often think about Pa. I missed him so.

Nights were especially lonely without Pa. Me and Ma played Rummy by the light of the kerosene lamp in the kitchen, while Jenny played on the floor near the stove with Mandy, her old rag doll, whose flattened body, bursting at the seams, looked like she had been through the wringer of our washing machine a hundred times. After cards, Ma would mend and I would sit in front of the stove, feet crossed on the warm pedestal of the oven door, playing sad western tunes on my dime-store harmonica. One night, I stopped playing and watched Jenny trying to close a hole in her doll's head with a safety pin.

If only I could get Jenny a new doll for Christmas. It was time for bed. We always went to bed early to save on kerosene.

The next morning a flyer on my paper bundle announced a New Customer contest. The prize was ten dollars. I entered the contest and went to six houses. No luck. Then I remembered what Pa said once about the law of averages. He said that if you try something ten times, you would succeed by the tenth time. By the end of the week, like a miracle, I had sold ten subscriptions. Visions of the wagon danced around in my head. That night I went to bed and made plans to sell more subscriptions the next day. I gulped down my oatmeal and toast and got ready for school. When Ma told me I couldn't go to school because of a snowstorm, I thought I would die. I pleaded and whined, but Ma said I'd catch my death of cold because I had no overshoes. Going to the kitchen window, inwardly cursing the snow, I knelt down and leaned both arms on the sill.

The dark narrow space between the window and the sill let in thin ribbons of ice cold air and snow dust with each gust of wind outside. Goosebumps covered my arms like cold chicken skin as I watched the storm get worse. I began thinking - making a plan. I waited until the old grandfather clock in the parlor chimed seven gongs so Ma wouldn't hear the squeaky doorknob turn from the pantry. I was out in the cold. A shimmering sheet of unbroken white glaze covered the snow. I delighted in making the first cracks on the thinly layered crust. The brittle sound broke the morning quiet as I made my way toward Nick's. Flickering street lamps made feeble efforts to shine through the misty fog-like snow. A horse-drawn milk wagon clippity-clopped and jingled past me, seemingly unaware of my presence.

"Jackie, what in tarnation you doin' out in a storm like this? Does your mother know you're out?"

"N-no Mr. Nick, ya see, this is the last day of the contest. I had to go out today."

Nick poured a steaming cup of cocoa in a cracked white mug from a blue porcelain pot.

"I'll pay you back Mr. Nick, soon as I get some money."

"Nah, no need t'pay for it Jackie, t'son me."

"Gee, thanks, Mr. Nick. Thanks a lot."

After I had warmed up a little, I left to deliver my papers. By the end of the route I had sold three more subscriptions. I was frozen stiff and scared to go home because I had disobeyed Ma.

"Where were you?" Ma yelled as I opened the kitchen door. "I was worried sick about you. Where have you been?"

"I had to go out today Ma, I just had to. It's the last day of the contest. I just couldn't stay home today."

Ma made me change into my flannellette nightgown and red felt slippers. As I sat in front of the oven Jenny fussed over me like a mother hen, struggling to cover me with her paiseley print patchwork quilt. A few days later . . . "I won! I won! Look Ma, it's right here in the paper. I won the ten dollars Ma!"

Ma and Jenny were so happy for me. I took the trolley to town right away to claim my prize. On the way back the trolley was packed, and I squeezed through to the back and balanced myself on a curved metal seat handle. The passengers swayed back and forth to the steady, rocking movement of the electric car. At the first stop the trolley halted abruptly, pushing people against each other, and the envelope slipped from my hand. When I went to pick it up someone had stepped on it as if daring me to take it. It was one of the tough kids from Collier's Corner.

"Gimme that," I yelled, "it's mine!" As I struggled to push his leg out of the way, I felt the cement-like muscles of his calves, but I kept shoving and yelling to the top of my lungs. The kid was embarrassed because everyone glared at him. He took his foot off the envelope, but before he got off the trolley he gave me a shove with his elbow. I shoved him back. When I got to Letourneau's I looked in the window to see if the wagon was still there. It was. I was finally going to get the wagon I wanted for so long. But next to the wagon was a beautiful mama doll dressed in a pale blue satin dress trimmed with white lace. She wore a bonnet to match, white rayon ankle socks, and black patent-leather slippers. Her large blue eyes shone like sparkling crystals under stiff black eyelashes. Purer than white celluloid teeth and shiny red cupid lips smiled whimsically. Soft blonde baloney curls hugged the sides of her rosy cheeks, and her outstretched arms and dimpled hands reached out to me. I thought about Jenny playing with Mandy, but then I thought about the wagon. I really needed that wagon. Maybe Ma could make Jenny a new doll for Christmas. I walked into the store.

I could reach the wagon on the back edge of the display window. The body was made of sturdy oak slats. It had bright red wheels rimmed with narrow black rubber tires, and a shiny black metal handle. I stroked its sides, its wheels, I moved it back and forth in admiration. I could see myself sporting it on my paper route. Then my eyes turned to the doll. I couldn't help thinking how happy Jenny would be to get such a doll for Christmas. Again I looked longingly at the wagon I had wanted for so long, but I reached for the doll. It cost eight dollars. I bought a snow paper-weight for Ma. I turned it over and watched the delicate snowflakes swirl and settle, petal-soft around a figure of St. Nicholas giving a gift to a little child. It reminded me of something Ma once said, "It is in giving that we receive." As I left Letourneau's I still yearned for the wagon, but I thought . . . maybe next year there'll be another contest.

Miraculous Medal Magazine January 1995

MERRY CHRISTMAS, OH YEAH!

'Twas the week before Christmas and all over town,
Everybody was stirring and running around.
The tree lights and carolers were a beautiful sight,
But a storm cast a haze on the wintery night.

And I in my Chevy on Madison Street,
Did fail to observe the cop on the beat.
A few feet behind there arose such a clatter,
I jammed on the brakes to see what was the matter.

When what to my wondering eyes should appear,
But a giant policeman coming up from the rear.
Ranting and raving and yelling so loud,
I felt like a nickle in the gathering crowd.

He swore up and down that he signaled to stop,
But the night was so dim that I saw not a cop.
A note from the registry brought me much dismay,
'Cause it said on the paper I refused to obey.

I knew when I read it I'd pay a stiff fine,
No need to appeal or to grumble or whine.
And to try to explain is a long losing fight.
Merry Christmas to all, and to all a Good Night!

(With apologies to Clement Clarke Moore)
The Open Door Newspaper 1979

HOW GREAT IT WAS

O Lord, my God, when I in awesome wonder,
Consider all the bills I made this year.
I see the frown, I hear the rolling thunder
When it is time to pay the bills, O dear.

So many times I often wish we pondered
And put less gifts under the Christmas tree.
When we were young we never ceased to wonder
At hand made toys, fruits, nuts, and candy.

In days of old, under the Christmas tree,
There were no frills, there were no bills.
Yet we were happy - happy as could be.
How great it was, how great it was.

Pungent Prayer Mediapolis News Frankfort IL 1977

LA ELECTRONIC MACHINE

An aspiring writer grew confident that
She could write a novel in two weeks flat.
The advertisements enticed her to
Buy a Word Processor - she followed through.

Booted up the system, installed the software,
Typed in the code and proceeded to stare.
By the time she was ready with all the above,
Her creative thoughts had flown like a dove.

She wondered and questioned and still doesn't know
Why La Machine blocked her creative flow.
She sold her Word Processor by placing an ad,
And returned to the method of pencil and pad.

ByLine Magazine January 1987

Mémé

(pronounced Mem-may)

The old rocking chair is empty today,
For Mémé no longer is in it.
She's off in her car doing volunteer work,
And rushes around every minute.

You won't see her watching late night TV,
And oft times her phone's off the hook.
Her iMac clickety-clacks through the night
For Mémé is writing a book.

Mémé still watches an occasional soap,
To relax in the midst of her day.
And as far as cooking and household chores,
She does that in a hit-and-miss way.

She's always looking for new things to do,
To make her life more enhancing.
And would you believe that at age sixty-five
She took to the stage and tap-dancing?

She isn't content with just sitting around,
A couch potato she's not.
And whenever a new opportunity knocks
You can bet she's hot to trot.

AH, THE ERASABLE PEN

Of all the great advances wrought by the hi-tech age,
Word Processing computers are holding center stage.
But I'm not one who can *create* at mechanical machines,
I have to write in long-hand first, and then I type full steam.

I used to waste a lot of time with re-writes thrown away.
I could not tolerate a page with proof marks in the way.
The paper I have wasted could build a tamarack tree.
I know I'm a perfectionist, but then again, that's me.

I purchased some *erasables*, my problem's in the past.
I'm not a slave to re-writes, I'm really free at last.
Why didn't I use pencils? They have erasers too.
To tell the truth I hate to rise to sharpen them, don't you?

I've since saved reams of paper. My rough drafts rate a ten.
The circular file is empty. Ah, the erasable pen!

ByLine Magazine May 1985

ADAM AND EVE

While leafing through the *A* book of our encyclopedia, our six-year-old son was fully absorbed with the pictures on each page. When he came upon a picture of Adam and Eve in the Garden, he pointed to it, and in a low monotone voice he said quite seriously, "Tarzan and Jane."

-The Family Digest Magazine 1963

WISE DECISION

Before entering a souvenir shop on our vacation, we decided we would limit ourselves to a one-dollar souvenir. I spotted a *fanny whacker* made of pine. I couldn't reach it so I asked our seven-year-old son to look at the price on the back. He looked, hurriedly put it back and said, "We can't buy it Ma, it cost ten-dollars."

WOULD YOU BELIEVE, PURGATORY?

Small son to father. "When we make big sins we go straight down, right Dad?"

"Yes." Replied the father.

"Well, when we make small sins," asked the son, "can we go sideways?"

HELLIFINO STREET

A teenage boy asked his big brother, "What's the name of the street that crosses Main at Webster Square?

"Hell-if-I-know." The brother answered.

Teenager. "How do you spell that?"

WISHING GAME

After blowing out the candles on his birthday cake, our six-year-old son announced that he'd been wishing for a horse since he was three-years-old and he never got one. Looking at the blown out candles with a grimace he muttered, "Cheap candles."

DOUBLY EFFECTIVE

Our six-year-old, having already lost his first baby tooth (top front) eagerly awaited the loss of the other tooth. We surmised it was because he would find a dime under his pillow when it happened. The day arrived. He came running with the tooth in hand and said, "Hooray! Now I can fit two straws there instead of one."

DISAPPOINTED

During the fifties, we attended a ceremony at our Cathedral where the Bishop was scheduled to give Outstanding Awards in Scouting. While busying ourselves with getting ready, our five-year-old said, "Gee, I can't wait to see him!"

The procession had almost come to an end. I happened to glance at our son and noticed he was craning his neck every which way in search of *him*. Then, to our utter embarrassment, he yelled, "Where's Joey Bishop?

-The Family Digest July 1964

SUSPICIOUS

After having punished my seven-year-old by making him stand in the corner, he turned around and with squinting eyes he asked, "Are you suu-re you're not my wicked step-mother?"

CLOUD NINE DWELLERS

After having tried and failed at rooting some philedendron slips, I was determined to try again and succeed. Soon they were my pride and joy. Three plants adorned the kitchen window, two enhanced the living room end tables, and three covered the divider.

During school vacation I was bedridden for five days and the kids took over the management of the house. When I was up and about I asked them, "Did anyone water my plants while I was sick?"

Five voices quipped in unison, "What plants?

****

"Two roads diverged in a wood, and I -
I took the one less travelled by,
and that has made all the difference."

-Robert Frost